Down The Highlands Way

Carlos de los Ríos

ELDRIDGE PRESS : 2011

Down the Highlands Way
Carlos de los Ríos

First Edition December 2011

www.therealcarlosdelosrios.com

ISBN 13: 978-1-938051-06-7

Published by
Eldridge Press
P.O. Box 894
Pacific Grove, California 93950

Printed in the U.S.A.

Table of Contents

dedicated to

my little fox

I saw her face when I came into the bedroom,
that redness in her cheeks scared me
I knew something had changed
something was gone now.
her, next to me, was all that made me calm,
and I instantly knew deep inside me
that words wouldn't be a factor here.
I stood there, all the color draining from my face,
and I wanted to go back,
skip over the last ten minutes and try
to be the me that I was in her mind only
moments before – only seconds before.
we didn't say anything there;
we just looked at one another;
her devastated and me – sinking
to a place I thought I had left behind so long before.
but I was wrong.
so, so very wrong this time.
could I ever have seen her face like that
in my worst nightmare?
if I had, I would never have let things get to
the awful land I'd walked us into.
a wind passed right through the very
middle of me and left me colder
than I remembered ever having been.
I still walk to that doorway
and hope sometimes that I'll get to play the whole
thing over because this time, I'd not let her down;
I just know I wouldn't.
but that's gone, baby, so, so gone.
all I want is for her to fix me
a steak sandwich, pack us a lunch
and make me take her rowing.
it was something she used to make me do;
take her out on the lake so we'd get

1

time by ourselves.
I look back and I see that I never grasped
how good I had it.
quiet lunches on the lake with her smile
changing my very trajectory;
I was a fool – more a fool than usual,
and now I lose little bits of my real self
every day – each and every day without her.
I'd move the whole of my silliness aside,
so desperate is my longing.
I have had women love me or think they were
meant to be with me.
but there's been nothing close to what we were;
not for me.
I'm beyond self-pity and beyond hope.
I'm an altogether shadow of myself;
a small, pathetic wanderer; lost in a bad loop.
the little rules she wanted to try to hold
over me that I resented so much at the time
seem like the closest I've ever been to true love.
and chances? she'd given me every last one.
I have no one I can blame but
that ridiculous face I see in the mirror
each cold morning without anything I want to do; be, see.
I am now at that point that I can't find
a way to any relieving levity or perspective.
a man knows when he's fallen on his own sword;
a fool knows when his joke has fallen flat;
a moron knows why the sky laughs at him
with thunderous roars – a deafening ringing in my ears.
I keep wanting to drive to her house
but I'm now something I have never been: afraid.
I am afraid I'll see her with someone else
and that I'd come unglued and simply hurt myself.
I'm not weak but my arms won't lift;
my eyes don't want to open at all;
sleep is dark, belief is false and I
don't have the will to hope for anything for anyone.
this darkness has me in a cave
banging about, scraping my face up,

tearing at my feet and clawing at my back.
it is possible I have broken myself;
actually taken the very fiber of me and ripped it up;
like someone who hates even the prospect of a sunrise.
we used to go to the beach
and watch these gorgeous birds of prey
doing their meanest work or we'd sit in her car
and just stare at the ocean
putting ourselves into a sweet, sweet trance.
but now I'm really beyond hating myself;
because even that would reflect some kind of a passion
and I have less than a weakness – I have disease
of the dizzying kind;
I want to stand but my feet are antsy;
I want to run but can't stand;
and I want more than anything
to simply go rowing with her on that lake
she first introduced me to.
it is an attack on my body and mind
where I am now.
it is something so empty and cracked
that I can't hardly eat or even drink water.
it's like I'm waiting to die or something.
it sounds so dramatic coming from me
but it is the truth.
not a truth but THE truth.
I gave up, to hurt her as I did;
but what I did to myself
I didn't fully comprehend until of late.
you really have to hate yourself, I think
to become what I am.
baby, please, please can we go rowing?
I will be in trouble soon –
I can just feel that in my energy.
I don't want to be with me.
I may have found the great vast emptiness
that maybe I've been heading towards
for such a long time.
you don't feel the wind resistance when you stand
like a stone column.

just to hear her laugh even one more time
I'd do just about anything.
my want is so enormous I have to think
of how I planted these poisonous seeds and
how I watered them so regularly.
not all gardens are green and blooming;
some are just stupid and fake.
I'd cry if anything was still in me.
now I miss even the things I thought I disliked
in her when we were together.
I just wish more than anything that I
get shot, that someone makes me hurt.
at least I'd be able to bash my own brains
apart back to the molecular level.
I'm on my own – it's like a doctor
performing mad experiments on himself.
I am increasing my pace to that terrible ledge
where I once was able to muster vigor or at least
a single reason not to just jump.
I just want to go rowing today, my love.
I'd give anything to see you look at me
the way you once did. Anything at all.
can we please go rowing?
please…
I just want to go rowing today;
I just want to go rowing with you…

same cop keeps knocking on my door,
the fucking asshole trying to get intimate with me
or some shit I can't fucking figure out:
the dog was barking, the car is parked strangely
and I had to remind him for the third time
I don't own a goddamn dog
and he's the asshole that gave me the last DUI
that took my license which made me sell my truck.
but he's at the door again tonight,
talking some crap about the garden hose
and a complainer next door;
it'd all be fine – if anyone even lived next door.
so I can't get this motherfucker figured out.
"you wanna come in, officer?" I ask.
"well…it is late…" he feigns an indifference;
"no shit, genius," I say, "you may have noticed the pajamas."
"right…" he says.
but the fucker comes on in
and then I offer him a shot of vodka;
he takes me up on the offer.
I offer him beer.
same response. he guzzles it down.
I'm scratching my head trying to get a hold of this one;
then after we finish watching our second comedy TV show
it hits me!!
me and fuckface went to high school together;
he was a skinny, pimply dipshit back in the day;
unlike now when he's a fat, pimply dipshit!
and he's been waiting for me to remember
I figure;
"Ralph," I start tentatively, testing the first name,
"you want another cold one?"
the moment I utter his name aloud,
I know I'm right.
that's it.

"sure thing, Andy," he replies with a big, warm smile.
I go get the beer
but I'm still shaking my head at Dumbo;
my fucking name's not 'Andy'!

I'd been dying to lick her asshole,
since the first time she'd pushed
those little secretary/librarian glasses up her nose
to get a better look at me.
it was all I could think of sometimes;
it would drive me nuts, that marvelous ass,
a magical power it had over me;
like the snake charmer's flute tune;
I was mesmerized and unable to take my eyes off it.
she's beautiful in every way
and the most pristine of bitches;
and maybe that's why putting my face gently into
her ass, between those amazing cheeks
had me dizzy and genuinely devout.
she attended a stupid class
that I had no right being in –
(I went, I think, at first,
because my parents having been such academics,
I didn't know what else to do with spare time
but go listen to pompous jerks talk endlessly
about lies they'd read about in
deviously dumb books – this was just before IPads
and tablets and e-readers – and as I had always done,
when a younger man, I sat in back;
always in the back of the class).
and she, unlike me, was serious and studious
and a real sight;
the kind of young woman that I think
poetry and painting was probably invented over.
so those serious-types always sit forward
in contrast to self-made dilettantes like me.
she wasn't a fancy girl with self-important airs,
but rather that very thing that could weaken me:
a real person – no pretentions or fake bullshit
anywhere about her.

7

maybe it made that asshole of hers even more desirable;
gave it a mystique that could keep my simple brain
running around and around a train track
built by the littlest boy inside me.
yes, I think it was her realness
that kept me transfixed upon her back.
and when I finally got what I'd desired
it was better even than I had built
the experience up to be;
our nights were passionate and dirty –
kisses and fucking and snuggling.
yes, snuggling.
and that moronic class kept me alive
because I got to sit behind her
every class session -
as the students seemed to settle into regular seats
day in – day out
like they'd been assigned to us;
though that wasn't actually the case.
the teacher went on and on
and I was able to somehow hear the lessons
because I'd found my Zen place
like it was where I'd belonged my whole
miserable, selfish, pathetic life;
this much I knew;
I was supposed to be there
sitting a few rows back but somehow,
always with a perfect view to my Heaven.
and because she wasn't a show-off
or an egocentric woman she wore jeans
almost always – her family lived up on a mountain
like farmers or horse people or something.
and I wasn't alone in my opinion of her ass;
when I was out smoking with other male students
I'd overhear their crass open talk;
and that meeting place of her arched back and her long legs
was noticed by others.
I never stop thinking of it,
even now I'm hoping, I think,
that she'll forgive my unfaithful

and petty ways
and lay again on my bed
on her stomach, face down in the pillow;
legs spread apart just so;
inviting me to worship that lovely, sensitive button
tucked away like a hidden treasure.
and I always felt bad for those jeans of hers
having to handle so much perfection.
and it wasn't too much – nor was it at all regular –
that holy ass;
it wasn't too cold or too hot – it was just right.

…and she'd write these long letters
that she'd never send to anyone;
a cold, drafty house with a harsh longing
jutting out and stabbing at the innards
of the ones she no more wanted around her
than she loathed; a belly-filling loathing.
it was a sustenance, that feeling,
that she kept tucked away from even herself;
a drawing room of her mind's enjoyment –
with visitors who hadn't called on her in a decade.
that special, ruby-encrusted pen
was more than her frail hands wanted
to have to handle but she had a singular determination
deep in her
deep below where she let even herself look;
a mean-spirited revenge on herself.
few people can equal the triumphant defeat
she was prone to revel in
morning after morning – her and that special pen.
a private little wasteland she treasured
like it was a prize she'd won and was going
to let everyone never know about.
she'd rise like one of her precious ghosts
without need of any alarm clock –
she a machine with a devil's purpose to get
a letter written each morning.
if it was cold, she'd get up.
if it was warm, she'd get up quicker.
but she always got up
always found her empty table lively
with hollow memories of a Neverland
she was trying to keep alive –
a flight of archaic fancy all her own.
and no one was allowed to see her write
these letters – these deeply personal letters

that no one was ever to receive.
and when her mint tea was finished
and the day's letter was finished
she'd go to a special drawer and pull out an envelope;
address it meticulously, lick it sealed
and put a stamp on it.
then she'd walk upstairs, go into the oldest room
of the house, walk to the chest, open it
and put the new letter in with the hundreds of others
that would all stay locked away there
with no hope for a parole from their
bizarre, neatly-tended graveyard.

what the fuck am I doing?
I'm becoming just like all the other idiots
in your life – wrapped around your finger.
does anyone win with you?
I'm really having trouble confronting something
that I think I now must face.
a reality that I have to accept
and even, strangely, embrace.
what was I thinking?
what have I been wandering this desolate land for, anyway?
I'm in the tent of my own design –
the kind that folds up the minute it rains,
the kind that you take back to the store.
I'm shaking my head,
unsure how I'll be on the other side of this.
unsure if I can even really utter the words aloud.
am I a fool?
you better damned-well-fucking-believe it.
I've always been lost on this one.
and now there's no way to turn my head away.
no way to swallow this horse pill nicely.
this one's stuck in my throat.
it was ever.
it was ever.
what a laugh at me.
it's a cheap, yellow-stained carpet
of a bad open-mic-night-of-a-day.
how am I still standing on this collapsing stage?
no one's laughing.
well, that's not exactly true, now.
there is one loud guffaw
that rattles around and around and around like
a quiet spider's squeal under the foot
of a mean/indifferent/cold child.
it's a flop sweat inside me.

I'm turning this way and that.
where is the cruel laughter coming from?
<you can't find what you already have>
a damp feeling that makes me want to run in circles like a rabid dog
gnawing at itself – infecting itself.
my head is down.
it simply won't come up.
I don't want to pick it up;
I'm going to have to get off the stage now.
I'm going to have to take my licks –
and I'm one tough critic of the kind of comedy
I've drop-kicked my ass into;
it's settling in on me;
I resisted all I could,
this awful thing.
I mean, I suppose I'M THE ONE laughing at the clown
I am now become.
I knew this. I did. I really did.
but denial is a wonderful thing:
a last tool for the lost.
a knock at my door and I run to answer.
I know exactly what I'm not going to find there.
whom I'm not going to find there.
and I pace and sweat and talk to myself – again –
again I'm muttering to myself.
<my eyes are soft>
I'll be alright – sure.
Sure.
drinks won't wash this away
and I can't even find the strength
to put the cup to my cracked lips.
how many ways did I know this but deny
what I was building like a handicapped carpenter
--toolbox missing and unsought?
doors slam in my head.
who will I be tomorrow?
I actually know the answer.
I just don't like it.
I'm fading out like the Invisible Man
when I stare at my damned front door.

but I know it.
I know it in my bones.
I know it in some place deeper than bones.
you aren't coming back.
ever.
it's the truth,
whether or not it's grim or grisly.
I can't keep holding on.
my grip's been slipping…
bit
  by
   bit
I have to let go of this rotted wood
floating in the middle of the open sea
and I have to swim of my own volition.
I have to find my long-dormant strength
to get me back to the shore.
I have to focus on the shore now.
it will help me to forget
that I was once in paradise.
I'll forget, yeah, right.
sure.

I've been holding my breath
since you called two weeks ago.
you phoned out of nowhere,
apologized to me for various reasons
and then said you'd be back
in California on December 30th
and that you'd call sometime thereafter.
well, it's January 5th and no call.
you said we'd discuss our future.
you said you needed me as a friend
even if we could not be lovers.
I haven't been able to work
or go out with friends since your call.
that damned fucking call
has me tip-toeing around the phone
praying it won't ring but hoping it will.
and strangely, if it does, I'm not sure
what I'll say to you.
I've been alone in this room so long
it's starting to seem normal.
I can't stand the stench of me;
the odor is offensive;
rotten eggs and dogshit blended-up with self-pity.
it's not one of my better days;
and I've had some pretty bad ones.
I want to break every single thing in this tiny room.
I want to go get arrested again but
I know that will just make me happy
and I don't know that happy's
in the cards for me this time.
you really made me into everything
I was bound to make myself into.
lick a tree branch;
eat squirrel guts;
file down my corneas with a rusty file –

stuff myself in a garbage bag and toss myself to
the assholes I convinced myself were
the multiple personalities in me.
everything annoys me and eats me alive;
doing nothing doesn't work.
working doesn't work.
I've been a ragdoll owned by a paint-chip-eating
Chinese baby girl that needs a good drowning.
<the dark is sleepy torture>
and we were never perfect;
we were never what I could handle.
or is that the bullshit I tell myself
all morning long as I wait for comfort that
I scared off a long time ago?
dripping cold with the fever sweats;
bumping into walls that aren't there;
finding treasure that has no worth –
not for me.
I'm all elbows up to my eyes;
a real sight, I bet, to the blind men
pointing at me with their indifference.
they all tell me it's better like this.
they don't lie very well.
but they're right.
or am I?
left and right are the same direction now;
a big-rig road kill sandwich with
extra loathing on my soul slaw.
I vacillate hourly between
hating you and loving you.
friends introduced me to a good woman,
hoping she and I would strike it off,
and though I went through the motions,
I was internally ignoring her after only minutes.
she was a pale attempt at you.
a hollow shadowy woman
who only made me angry.
angry at myself, not her.
it's odd to imagine you
with your cell phone, out with

the girl pals; not answering.
hey, your caller I.D.'s paying off.
I just wish you hadn't called,
and I wish you'd just go the hell away.

Have you found a way
to make yourself prettier
than you were?
Are you crashing your life
into the cement like me
or are you fine?
Nothing has happened.
It's all cool to you.
Don't expect a lot
when you come strolling by, baby.
You are doing this to us.
Not me.
Your drama must be entertaining to someone.
There's got to be a Tony Award-watching audience
wearing fur coats and chugging champagne
in your head.
I wanted this: "Us" this.
I really wanted this.
And that's not easy for a prick like me to say;
not easy to parking lot-accident fake it.
It was something good, I thought.
It was worth more than I'm worth;
and maybe that was the problem.
I bolted doors and pulled curtains
to find that place in the little world
I came to not just enjoy and want;
but need.
I don't think I'll be coming this way
any time soon.
I might be standing there
but there's nothing there;
like I fell asleep at the wheel again;
wrapping another car around another telephone pole.
I'm not home.
I'm on a sabbatical from being genuine now;

I'm worn down to not much more than
what I started out as –
and I never thought I'd be back in that place.
It's been so long that I don't remember
coughing up my life over this.
I slap little kids and toss dogs off cliffs;
I hunt for an alcohol with a proof that can't exist.
"Can I please get a 300 proof Maker's neat?"
No?
I'm the bottom of a shoe now;
the hole-ey shoe of a gibberish king
in a slanted room of mirrors.
I like being this awful now;
can't find what was okay about me.
A gleeful, smoking car crash of a mouth
is what I use to drop piss on the path ahead of me.
So I'm just saying,
a door is closing and I won't open it
once it shuts.
I'm not on my knees anymore
and I suspect you are,
so it makes me wonder
why the world spins so twisted.
Nothing I have done
and nothing I have read
prepared me for this moment.
Left on my own with no food,
and my enemies closing in all around.
No more allies and no more kisses
for a knight trying to fight darkness.
I've known too many liars
to be fooled by your words, sweetheart.
There is nothing repentant in you.
There is no sense of the folly
that you topple over and lay at
others' feet daily.
There is only the beauty
that you see when you look
for hours and hours and hours
on end into that silvery mirror.

the trees sway gently – deceptively
giving off the impression that all is calm
the wind has died down
and a flock of gulls settle;
there are no cars moving around
at society's required light speed.
an old woman across the street
turns off her television set
as her husband closes the 'fridge door.
the sound of the toilet refilling
the water tank comes to a stop.
the light at the corner turns to red,
the street lamps that were flickering steady and hold.
no cell phones are ringing.
no airplanes overhead.
no words.
no people.
they sleep only because they
don't know what I'm about to do.

what I do to you I won't feel sorry for,
and when I bring it, you will feel it.
I honestly wonder if you'll survive it.
will you have the strength
to survive me
Me Me Me
a full attack, with teeth bared?
it feels like a pompous question
but somehow a realistic one too.
when I bring it to you
there will be no mercy,
forever to be at war.
I know this as I do what I do.
I suspect you didn't have any idea
that I could strike back.
what did you think?
that I'm a fucking saint?
I'm a man. a real, human man.
my pulse is up and you will be feeling me.

sometimes I can only think of your hands
your perfect, small hands in mine
your soft hands running along my arm
making everything good
what a thing, "good" –
to have some of that when so much of the day
and so much of the night isn't.
when there are hours and days and weeks
that go by with nothing worthy of note
how small and amazing a thing that your hands
could bring so much to me
give so much meaning to all the miles
I've walked over the years.
it isn't like you ever had to try
to change everything for me
you just did
with no effort, with no warning
and after a while I think I came to expect
to feel that way all the time
never giving a thought to the fact that
you weren't a given,
you were a gift, a miracle, a laugh
in the face of human frailty
your hands just running along my arm,
or up my neck to scrub at my hair
were the very stuff I'd been seeking
a whole lifetime without knowing it.
it's stunning to me now
how I could just let those hands,
those special hands made seemingly just for me,
slip out of my own
without having moved Heaven and Earth
to hold on.
I look at women's hands as I pass them
on the street or in the stores

or at work or in the parks
and I think how many, many hands
there are in this big world
that weren't meant for me

MY NARDS

the one time I really got knocked down
by a guy in a fight
I think I ruined the whole thing
for him.
in fact, I'm pretty sure I did.
I was at the Bulldog Pub on Lighthouse Avenue
as usual,
talking to friends and drinking beers
when a man I didn't know at all
tapped me on the shoulder,
a pissed-off look on his face
that made me put my mug down.
"you were hitting on my girlfriend, let's step outside, dude,"
the odd man sprayed.
I wiped my glasses of his saliva and picked my mug back up;
"fuck off, asshole, because if you mean
that little Asian girl in the leather pants,
she came up to me and asked for my friend's phone number,"
I responded disinterestedly.
"no. no. no way," he managed to get out.
"yes. yes. yes way. she did try to get
with another dude that's not you, but it wasn't me," I said.
"this is bullshit! you're a dead man!" he said.
"this is bullshit but your problem is with
your two-faced girl who wanted my friend's number."
he thought it over a moment.
as I was telling the truth, he was confused.
being fairly drunk, he just went back to Plan A –
"this is bullshit! you're a dead man!" he repeated,
this time with a noticeably lesser degree of confidence.
"okay," I said. I don't really mind fighting
so in an odd way it sounded like a gas.
we went outside, in front of the pub,

and he asked me again about his girl.
I repeated what had actually occurred and it really
seemed to make him sad.
"it's too bad, man, but I'm still okay with fighting,"
I offered as a consolation to his obviously declining
sense of his own manhood, "…if you want…"
he looked back inside the pub, saw his girl flirting
with yet a third man and so decided to take me up
on my generous offer.
"let's do this, asshole! you hit on my girl!"
"we already went over this," I continued, "but if
that's what makes you happy…okay, man."
he shook his head strangely trying to work up
his anger again.
he looked back in the bar, saw his girl kissing
a complete stranger to either of us
then turned his attention back to me.
"I'm gonna knock you on your ass," he yelled at me,
only half-heartedly.
I shrugged my shoulders indifferently
and he sort of closed his eyes but did
manage to lay a good punch or two to my face
so I went down to the pavement.
I was about to compliment his punching speed
when he looked again at his girl who had now
sandwiched herself between two men, unknown by either of us,
once again, the little lonely thing.
so the mad, sad guy standing over me huffed and puffed
almost like a cartoon Yosemite Sam
and then he revved up and kicked me in the groin.
he really nailed me, too;
I screamed out in pain.
"fuck! Jesus, fuck!" I hollered and coiled up.
"ha! I just got you, asshole!
I'm going to kick you in the nards again!" he gloated.
but I chuckled
which caught him off guard.
the glee on his face started to dissipate
and was replaced by a perplexed look.
I giggled then and this was not to his liking.

I asked, "did you just say, 'nards'?"
he was confused then.
"you just said, kick me in the 'nards'," I snickered
still laying on the ground.
"…yeah?"
"nards. nards?" I couldn't hide my widening smile.
he really didn't like the direction our talk was heading, now.
"no one's told me they'd kick me in the nards since…
man…like…fifth grade," I started laughing.
"no. I -- I didn't say…that," he stammered
but a pretty blond smoking a menthol
on a bench in front of the pub
chimed in, "yeah…you did. you said you'd
kick him in the nards."
when she started laughing it enraged the guy,
so he yelled at me, "if you don't shut up I'll…"
"what? kick me in the nards?" now I was guffawing uncontrollably
and the blond was laughing so hard she dropped her cigarette.
the guy looked back inside and saw "his girl"
kissing the second unknown fellow inside the bar.
it was all too much for him
and as he ran off down the street
I know I saw him crying

I have been polite and respectful too long,
and I will not make that mistake anymore.
not sure exactly when I broke my own back;
not sure how I fused it together again with
storms like these raging all around.
I am not sure of much anymore;
at least, not the things I once was certain of.
but this feeling welling up in me
is a strong one – a consistent one –
and that is new.
a "new" I like,
a new that drives me.
my fingertips tingle when I push my seat back to stand up now;
my feet grounded in a manner I'm unaccustomed to;
but this…this…is here to stay.
I am not going to be afraid to disappoint you
if I take an action you would deem radical.
I'm no longer in a position to care
and that is very dangerous to you, I guarantee.
I have lost so much more than
you will ever be able to know
and this fact puts me in a unique position.
they say that any person
willing to sacrifice their own life
has a decent chance at killing any other
human being on the planet;
even if the target is a president,
or a highly-guarded pop star.
no one is safe from utter freedom's attack.
someone with no strings flies into battle.
so when you see the whites of my eyes
you'd best turn and run because I'll be harsher
than you ever knew of me
as I lay those who stand up to me down.

did you forget that I am just a man?
did you think I was merely this entertainment
entity that is available for hire?
do you think that because I'm a writer
I won't kill, shoot, murder and pillage?
if you put me in the right position
I'll do anything any other junkyard dog would.
if you want to talk to me that way
that's a very interesting choice.
it actually fascinates me
that you could miss that every animal
will kick, bite, maneuver and claw
before being taken down.
you have failed me.
again and again you have done nothing
to help us.
and now, I'm forgetting whether or not you matter.

You will hide now, I see.
That makes me laugh,
to think of you afraid to speak to me;
afraid of what I'll say next.
Are my words that terrorist?
Are my thoughts so destructive?
Are my opinions shrapnel-laden?
I am floating with the river's strength
in letting go of my memory of you.
I don't want the feeling
of what it was like to be with you
to leave me.
But it is.
I'm clinging to it desperately.
But it will go
whether I will it to or not.
It is not entirely in my control.
So stay hidden, uncalling, unreceptive, unavailable.
It suits you.
Strangely, being without you
is a lot like being with you.

you wouldn't believe all the bad things
I've been doing since we broke up,
you would be stunned at what I've done
-at the way I've been treating women.
I'm as immature right now as a boy.
I want revenge on you
and instead I'm taking it out on various
women who've been drawn into my life.
I'm not saying rude things or insulting them
but I am lying to them all.
I am making each one believe
that they are all I can see.
I am fooling them into kissing me
and conning them into sleeping with me.
when I'm through I'm going to leave
six or seven hearts torn up
and bleeding all over the place.
and still I wonder what I'll destroy next
to distract myself from your absence.

this is a different ending to our story
than I would have guessed at.
nothing really worked out at all
the way either of us hoped.
we knew we were facing an uphill struggle
but we went forward even so;
hold a fire in your hand long enough
and you will hold nothing again.
I can't say what would have fixed us
or how many of the king's men
it would have taken to put us
back together again.
I just know you can't ever
have appreciated me.
let's walk back to the beginning
where we can put on a happy face
and make believe at hope.

I'm going to let loose now
and fire at will at every target
I've been meaning to hit.
I once told you that being with you
kept me from smoking pot
and kept me from drinking tequila
and kept me from fist fighting.
well...
you're gone!
so there is no more restraint on me;
I'm a mean, ass-kicking SOB again.
I'm the drunk talking back to the cops.
I'm the guy with his stereo too loud,
sitting just outside a Republican rally.
I'm the guy drinking the bar out
of certain brands of liquor
and slapping people who sit too close to me.
I'm the guy parking my car
on the neighbor's front lawn
and puking in his unlocked cock-compensation Porsche.
I'm the guy kicking in the back door
when it takes too long for the homeowner to answer;
I'm the guy stealing people's mail
just to read into their privacy.
I'm the guy burning down the banks
just because their neon signs annoy me
and throwing hamburgers at college athletes
just to see them break their precious hands
trying to punch me – a faster demon than
they think they're dealing with.
I'm the guy YouTube-ing the boss' illicit affair
to Christmas jingles and berating priests
for their psychotic, pedophilic preachings.
I'm the guy punching a hole in your door,
smashing in your car windshield

and running you over just 'cuz you
looked at me crossed.

she's got me distracted
in just that right way,
got me staring too long
and turning shades of red.
she's so wildly beautiful
I can only think of giving in
to all the temptations she offers.
I'm not even supposed to be
having any kind of personal life.
I'm supposed to be a soldier;
no women until the war is over.
but just when I was committed
to the warrior's life
she shows up to remind me
what I'm even fighting the war for.
so I'm in a terrible mood;
I'm pissed off, grieving over
dead friends, thinking of impending death
and all my friends who suffer,
but even so, looking at her, I'm all grins.

it's been a long time since I felt this way
and now I think many people will feel it.
this will not stop here,
that much is certain.
it's a wind flowing through me and past;
it's an energy that many have avoided;
it's where the businessman's eyes go
when he wants to murder the Ferrari dealer
for teasing him all life long.
it's the sun on the backs of the serial killers
who celebrate their dominance of Juarez.
it's the gunshots from FBI agents killing
killers who don't know why they first killed.
it's the birds shitting on your new Mercedes
as you pull in to pick up your hot date.
you can dance left – you can dance right
but the monsters intended to crunch your bones
will have their day whether you like it or not.

you find ways to turn your head
and not have to see the bloody bodies
laid out in the wake of your passing;
you are crying false tears
that you want the press to photograph.
sadness consumes your every thought --
you are not pleased with yourself
you know you have treated me poorly.
you feel so low when you look
in the mirror that you want to
run out and binge on food or liquor;
all your carefully laid-out plans
are crumbling because the world
cannot be easily categorized and organized.
you wanted me to be so very simple
and I am sorry I disappointed you in that.
but I really think you are in
for a big shock as the people in your life
all turn to you and ask why you treat them like you do.

"I've never had a boyfriend I saw once a week,"
she said to me as we sat at the club.
dance music blared over the system,
"you want to see me more," I said.
"no. yes. do you?"
"of course."
"are we...real?"
"I don't know. I think so."
"do you hope so?"
"what do you think?"
"I'm here..."
"yes you are. and you really are a very...very..."
"yes?"
"well...you know what I'm saying."
"no. I don't"
"well...I'm here too..."
"well."
"well."
"don't repeat me
and wipe that look
off your face," she glared and then
took a long sip of her apple martini.
"we've been dating for three weeks."
"right. and I'm used to someone
falling in love with me and wanting to
spend all their time with me."
"like how often?"
"every day."
"every day?"
"every day."
"wow...okay."

he came to me a screaming little boy
a screaming beauty of a small future man
a little piece of the motherlode
gold in my hands – a painting famous already
and I freaked out at the responsibility;
he seemed like he wanted to scream
until he was ready to pass out.
I decided to hold him
through the screaming and the long night
and the next long night
and the next long night
and so on and so on;
before long the crying lessened
and he even started acting "normal",
he wanted to play with me constantly;
he had no sense that playtime was supposed to end,
he could literally run around like crazy
and play silly games
and hide and jump and smash and crash
and roll and hop and leap and crawl
and rumble and tumble and flail
and grind and spin and spin
and twirl and wail and tromp
and climb and maul and stare
and destroy and growl and scream –
oh boy could he scream and scream
the kind of scream that could make
a sad man smile and a mad man relax --
until he'd run out of steam.
then he'd crawl into his special bed
and fall asleep for an hour or two
before waking to start it all over again.
and now he is a man, with no fear left
and he sits next to me,
talking only occasionally

comforting me –
the only thing truly
keeping me from screaming.

You have absolutely wrecked me;
taken me from the sky to hell.
You have made me question myself.
That is something I have rarely done.
I'm stuck in a mud pit, unable to move.
You have succeeded in spreading
your stupid fucking depression:
your overly-glorified emotion drain.
I'm alone in the garden.
I have cried for four days
and see no end in sight.
Yeah, me...crying...tears and shit, man.
I am all over the place – unstill.
A warble and a wobble and a flop to and fro.
There is a rage in me that is right on the surface.
It's a bubbling red rage screaming
in white hot silence.
I'm vibrating so fast
at such a tremendous frequency
it appears that I'm sitting still.
My anger is so rooftop popping
it looks to the casual observer like a party.
I am pissed off all the time.
I'm far beyond irritable.
What I am is something else.
I am a walking fight.
Guy walks up to me and smiles
like he fucking knows me –
he's probably heard some story about me
and he's going to try to make friendly.
"Just talk to me
I dare you," I whisper
just quietly enough that I know he can't hear me,
but I also know he hears my tone –
what my insides are "saying" loud and clear.

He gets up slowly, frowns and walks away.
See.
Do you see?
You have twisted me now
into something I don't recognize.
I have always known how to behave
but now I find myself unglued;
I am coming apart at the seams;
You left me to drown,
saying that my splashing was annoying.
You crushed me down so low
that I have indeed changed.
And mostly for the worst, it's fair to say.
I am now more than willing to find flaws with people
and then more than excited to point them out loudly.
You have actually killed me;
The "me" you knew doesn't even exist
anymore; he is dead and rotted
on a pile of steaming compost.
It is true "I" have died.
Parts of me are gone and I don't
know where they went or
what roads they took to leave me.
I am not people's friend anymore.
I don't love or hate anymore.
I have no feeling in me at all for them.
I couldn't care at all if they
are made suddenly wealthy or made into
human sausage by a serial killer.
People joke with me that I should smile.
I just need to "chill out" they say.
Well fuck them and fuck you.
Fuck anything that annoys or irritates me
from here on out, baby.
Fuck all your bullshit
and fuck all your lies.

...by pulling out a cigarette with a shaky hand
and lighting it deliberately...slowly;
her nails are gnawed raw –
that's her way – her nervous tick
that she's never been able to get rid of.
she even does it when she's at the dinner table,
other diners being put off their meals
by her constant fingernail chewing
and strange erratic smoking.
"do you really have to smoke at the table
while we try to eat, baby," her mom asks.
"you want me back on the street
sucking dick for crack rock, Mom?!"
"of course not sweetheart,
but your dad has asthma and Mary isn't
feeling all that well either."
"fine. I get it."
she stands up and walks out in her pink heels;
her black, torn-up skirt revealing far too much;
then she's back in the room again
her tears streaking her cheap mascara
all down her dramatic face.
"I hate you!"
no one at the table stops eating.
No one.
this is a usual Friday night at their house;
then she walks out the front door
slamming it hard, behind her.
everyone eats, bread and salt and wine
passing around the table.
then, as if on cue, she's back, opens the door,
"Dad...can you give me a ride?"
her father stands up.
to the table, "be right back."
he walks out with her, drives her downtown

and drops her off at 'hooker corner';
the other ladies smiling and waving at her
with a friendly familiarity.
her father leans out the window --
"your mother works tomorrow morning, sweetie
so when you come in, be sure to keep it down,
especially with the porn and the music, okay?"
before she can answer, he speeds off;
then back to the table and he sits down;
"Mary, can you pass me those potatoes,
they are just...*so* good."
"yams, honey, they're yams."
"great stuff," he smiles at her and digs in.

"go ahead and touch it," she indicated her ass,
and I hesitantly did so, her being a real friend;
and not someone I'd ever had sex with
or tried to – too hard.
I put my hand on that jean-covered backside and felt it;
"that is really nice," I said to her sincerely;
I kept feeling around, under, up her lower back
and down her inner thighs.
"this is so crazy," she blushed –
and this was not the kind of girl who blushes –
(and I can say that because she really is my true friend).
"I agree…but I'm in an honesty phase right now
so I'm not going to say that this is anything but –
just…fucking great. Not the part about me feeling you up,
but the part about us just doing this…
without either of us feeling any kind of guilt."
she laughed lightly, "yeah…I know. I am really turned on
and…I know we're not going to fuck or anything and—"
"that's what I was just thinking. your brother is my
closest friend – I couldn't probably even get hard –
not enough to really make it worth anything –
I mean – his angry face popping into my head
while we went at it," I said.
"don't stop, though, okay?" she asked quietly.
"this is so weird but so cool," I looked her in the eyes;
her breathy smile told me she was thinking the same thing.
"you are really gorgeous and you have lost not a damn thing
over the years," I said.
we'd been friends at that point for nearly 25 years;
since grade school in our small, hick hometown.
"can I smoke a cigarette and you just keep…keep…doing that?"
I was turning red in the face, "yes. I don't want to do any
more than this…but I don't recall ever being this –
alive…really-really," I managed to get out like a grade school kid.
"should we take your pants off and I can play with your dick?"

I was physically up to the suggestion
but I paused in responding – a long pause.
"I don't know," I answered truthfully.
"let's do it – get naked – play – no fucking –
just play like kids…" she said, looking into my eyes.
I couldn't get my mouth to answer her.
I just kept rubbing her – and not her crotch –
just her womanly features – attributes.
she didn't say anything back either.
she smiled and got on all fours on my couch;
I ran my hands over her (clothes on)
for another half hour.
she posed about like a model
and I spanked her a few times, gently;
then we stood up and hugged so tightly;
so so tightly.
then we giggled and I kissed her neck once,
her cheek once, and her forehead twice.
then we sat down and watched a really bad comedy;
neither of us able to laugh;
and I got up, poured us beer mugs of red wine
and we talked and made fun of all the idiots
we shared in common
before simply relaxing and enjoying our evening
like the real friends we still are to this very day.
we never talked about it again
but any time we are alone
she gives me that look
and my hands run around her pants
for as long as we can remain unseen by others.
it's unlike anything I've done with anyone before
and I can't see it happening with anyone else.
it just is what it is and we both adore
one another even more than we ever have.
I think it just makes us feel young
and un-dirty; just…young

…over battles wreathed in demon-flame and fear
it is the foolish nature of men to hold on;
to keep close a faith even when falling to depths
heretofore believed nonexistent and the stuff of fables.
roars and choruses dripping nightmare loss
on foul winds cresting over mountains;
ropes burning my hands to the bone
after endless days and nights lost in the darkest
of darknesses – creatures unknowable and unwanted everywhere;
and the grappling internal so very intense;
biting into my flesh and taking hold
of the very core of my being.
crying and begging is no use here,
not now after all the infinite steps taken;
one step right
two steps left
three steps nowhere;
a treachery within myself against myself
the real battle, more and more likely unwinnable
by the light of nights brighter than day.
wasteland fires and fogs
the undead shambling to and fro
brainless but determined with specific intentions
built on ages of shame and reflections born
out of the halls of deepest keeps.
the unsaved eat up the lore they've been fed
by magicians whose sleight of hand
could marginalize even the keenest eyes;
none so tainted teasing like these beasts
content to wallow in the rivers of blood
they drink freely from –
bone and bile all a pile
needling whispers of gallantry held close
to the chests of men who've given in
inch-by-inch, step-by-step

until what I see before me is all that remains.
infestation and charm all the same here
below where God herself wonders of the future
and if it even exists;
a time after time was to be but a dream in the eye
of children wiser than the waters;
pronouncedly brilliant and animal by nature;
gargantuan in their infinitesimally micro quality;
a testament to the end of the concept of endings;
proof irrefutable that to need proof is indication
of a deeply false inner-working.
I am attacked and safe in such war;
untouchable because of my utterly mortal being.
puppets here are more real than "free" men
convinced that what they have seen is worth
reporting to others of their kind;
a puzzle already laid out solved
like rain joining into an ocean without liquidity;
gregarious indifference the law of a prison
I only now come to see that I constructed
cell by ion – protein by wish;
a call from the mountains under thought itself.
my heart races as it has been programmed to do
under such gloriously frightening circumstance;
the knots in my stomach tied by hands of they
of the worlds of the disembodied – rulers of nothing
like real and true "kings" were meant to be.
calculating for death is beyond foolish –
especially in a place where life itself is mere illusion
and where the union of friendship is the only truth.
it is there that the monsters lose whatever power
we have given them in our penultimate ignorance.
and so it is there that I shall rest these tired bones;
away from all I put over myself –
regions of hatred now withered by a new way;
a new way that's been waiting for me
since before I was;
since before before.

You have harassed me, tussled with me,
marginalized me and insulted me.
You have spat on me
and made me crawl through shit.
You have wronged me
and taken advantage of any forgiving nature.
You have abused my kindness.
You have taken advantage of me.
You have laughed at my expense.
But no more, bitch.
Not anymore, fucking bitch.
Now I will do as I please.
I will listen less and talk more.
I will do the things I've always wanted to.
Your pathetic gestures of reconciliation
mean nothing to me, stinking motherfucker.
Step off fake monster or I'll slap your face red, black and blue.

let me adjust your jaw
so that it sits to the side.
let me have my way
with your collarbone and arms;
I'll snap you like a twig
and leave you burnt like a roach.
you've been signaling planes
acting like you know where
everything should be put,
but in reality, sweetheart,
you are more lost than
the ultra-religious we used to hate.
we sing out chants that
fall on deaf ears
that belong to people who
want to bury their heads
in a deep desert sand.
walk around, darling, and inhale deeply
your manicured stench

I need so much more money
than I have right now – it's sick!
I could use so much more dollar-power a year,
I'd burn it in no time flat,
the way these women out here
in the big Los Angeles have me
all twisted around them.
hatred is a many-faceted jewel
dropped from your anus
like your hair and your lips were something special;
it is a town made from the fake bullshit
Hollywood has gifted the world;
beauty – what a word.
what a fucking word.
these lost girls torn up inside by their
rapist fathers and abusive brothers
seek a revenge on an enemy they cannot see
and barely even believe in anymore.
it has a spell over them;
an incantation guttural and in a tongue lost
over the ages.
it is not anything but garbage
left out in a hot sun – wafting a foulness
from one continent to the next
like troll dung smeared across the faces
of their Chanel souls – nothing there –
nothing at all but falseness eating away
bit by bit at the very ones they rob
over and over and over; maybe thinking
souls are endless wellsprings of black meat –
rotted meat with maggoty spicing to tickle their tongues
to a vicious delight – a neon, Vegas, billboard reality.
women these barely are – and only in shadow;
and that shadow is ever-growing – ever-nearing
its true purpose – to seed the lands with char.

they want rings, houses, babies,
clothes, jewels, vacations and parties; endless, pointless parties.
it's enough to make any man
lose his mind and his wallet.
I've watched millionaires wince as
they see the latest dinner check arrive.
$600 for two people- with no drinks!
that's common in LA and with
this bullshit, even knowing of this Bush economy, that's…
that's…just stunning -- really stunning.
none of these women are a very good match
for me – it's getting clearer and clearer.
I'm just masturbating by dating them.
I'm just a stupid, dumb man led by his dick.
hell, the sex ain't even that great.
isn't that something now?
model – The Four Seasons on Doheny – X – all night -
and the sex is sterile, boring, unsatisfying.
(yet, a sweet woman with no airs
and a down-to-earth vibe really
wanting you, can drive you nuts
in just that perfect way.
what times they were before I fell into this trap.)
gorgeous women are a debilitating injury here.
I need Bill Gates' expense account
so I can expense these "dates"
that are nothing but big ol' money pits.
love is a four letter word here.

small hopes crowded in dark alleys
with the warplanes of doubt bombing away while
winter cold freezes the rivers of trust
making us look at one another in that way
the way
a way untold by waves covering grief;
bystanders are jaw-agape at us
and the photographers are loading film;
prepping their digital frameworks
for an end of time foretold but false and comic.
no one could have seen this coming,
and most ironic if you think about it,
of the none who could have never predicted this,
the ones closest to the fire
were the ones with least warmth of sight
and I can imagine not a one able to foresee this,
least of all you or me.
it's not just any old romance that can generate
all these myriad problems so fucking quickly.
and so by these conditional standards
I'm certain this,
this that we have on a pedestal before us,
is a grand love.
love on a massive scale
parameters unbound and gloriously unknowable;
don't be your doubting self. not today.
today be new
today be the old you
be of the real today you know true, deep in you,
today let your guard down;
let it down for me,
so that we can climb together
so that we can see as one
so that mountains appear to us as the dirt clods
they really are,

if we want them to be.
we didn't make these limits
we aren't bound by them
unless we believe our unseeing eyes
and give them power they wait for us to allow;
I never liked walls, was not the best carpenter
I never saw a barrier that made me slow
and I am asking here now, today, of you,
that you work from intuition, not learned facts
and inculcated bastardizations of what we may make
if we just have the strength to disbelieve in flesh
and to show no respect to stone and mortar --
climb over the walls with me,
swim across their ridiculous shark-infested moat
and let's run away, free, across the open fields
hand in hand
unafraid

she only eats filet mignon and lobster
and when she saves up enough,
she's going to Europe to travel
for an "indefinite period" -
and when she decides to go,
she tells me,
she'll be gone, just like that!
as easy as the snap
snap –
of fingers - that's how it'll be
when she's finally out of here.
she's got a boyfriend
but she's flirting with me,
letting me see her form
as she slinks about on me.
she's got her arms crossed
like she's really annoyed
but she laughs at all my jokes,
even the ones I know aren't funny.
and she's pitching this idea of hers
or that - always selling.
she's got on fancy, expensive jeans
that hug her form exquisitely.
but the see-through expression on her face
tells me that she's really confused.
she's selling too desperately
to convince a stone-eyed and intentional outcast like me;
she's using too many words and not even the right ones,
not to move a shithead-by-choice like me;
she has a special fire sale
but I'm not cynical –
I'm the one whose cold eyes the cynics
don't want to meet
for fear of being exposed as dramatists
thinking this world is nothing but

a stupid fucking stage.
Shakespeare – or whoever faked his name –
was full of shit.
this world ain't no fucking stage –
it's real – it's so real;
that's what the cynics don't get;
cynics like her –
that there is no playwright and no actors,
it's all – even the illusions – it's all
real.
now that's some hard shit to look in the eyes;
what if this did count?
all of it.
no timeouts, no score, no winners, just this
that we know
not what we see, hear or feel with our bodies
but the other thing –
that's what she doesn't like about my smile,
its loving acceptance and unconditional admiration,
its simple and un-profound presence.
this long journey didn't turn out
as she expected it to
and now she's beginning to panic.
she's developing odd, neurotic ticks.
she scrapes and scratches at her
once-perfect cheeks until they bleed
and scar in a most telling way.
I say little to her which makes things worse,
I just have this face,
and this look on this face
that doesn't want anything from her
but needs everything
like all the people behind all their faces do.
she wants me to show her a good time
and then wants me to vanish at midnight, like a good boy.

she's got her umbrella out but it's not raining
and she talks to an invisible friend,
in a made-up language no one can follow.
birds could roost in her messy hair
considering how long she can stay totally still;
she gets this dried-white saliva residue
in the corners of her mouth.
her father pays for her glorious bungalow
and she stays deep behind its gates;
the door has five locks on it.
she never ventures out except to
go to the local museum to see an exhibit.
usually she's escorted from the premises
the first time she spits at a painting or sculpture;
the guards freak, grab her, but then
seeing her crazy eyes figure she's retarded
so they guide her out forcefully but politely.

I'm not afraid of letting go anymore.
I've gone so far that there is no
going back now.
it's like mariners who've sailed out past
half their food supply
toward an uncertain shore.
I'm bent to the ground in pain
and still I find myself trying to stand.
I am now drinking regularly
and that is odd for me.
I seem to be in a bad mood
all the damned time.
it's like there's no escaping
that horrible mood that puts
the most sour look on my face;
it waits for me patiently

don't break out your fine china for me,
I'm just here for peanut butter and jelly.
I don't want to find shelter
from your malevolent hurricane.
I am content to sit in my seat,
a good, docile little boy,
and take all the rotten tomatoes hurled
right into my face with force.
I'm not asking for a Presidential pardon
for all the bullshit I brought
down on your head.
I'm just asking for some reality up here.
give me some goddamn reality.
just feed me, don't serve me,
I wasn't even sure whether or not
I'd get out of bed this morning

is this my moment?
I can't even look up to see.
I can only push forward.
I can only sweat and wince
in pain as I push through.
how do you know when
the lights of history are
shining down on you?
how do you begin to behave
when you think that
all your actions may be
poured over later in detail?
analyzed by brainy people
who will attribute so much
more to your behavior than was there.
I can't be sure if the lights
are on me or are just beside me
and are so bright
that they've confused me.

you wanted fame
but only got infamy,
you craved diamonds
but only got the heist bust,
you sought justice
but only got hammered;
and time stood against you,
sucking air from your lungs.
you thought you'd buy art
but got wall decorations instead,
you were inclined to watch TV shows
only to find ads for the movies,
you went to the desert
but got rained out.
and wisdom twirled you around,
leaving others wondering
if you'd ever walk again.
and you wanted to catch my attention
but instead fired up my obsession.

no one wants to walk with her
across that rickety bridge
and people are leaving her side
and running for the hills,
they fear her anger
and are taking cover where they can
by splattering her opinions all over
the walls of her friendships;
she revealed some disturbing
thought patterns that many of us noticed:
she told us she'd killed her last boss
and hid his body in a warehouse storage.
she told us he'd called her
a "beaner" so she shot him in
the parking garage that evening
and concealed his corpse.
she said she knew she could
trust us with her secret
and winked at us as she walked out the door

she'll be out partying until 4AM
and when she gets home she'll stumble
up the stairs and fumble with her
keys and the lock for five minutes.
then she'll go straight for the wet bar
and get herself a tequila shooter night cap.
she got arrested last week for being
drunk and disorderly at a children's parade;
she knocked the drum line down
by running her old Buick into them;
she went right through a police barricade.
poor kids went down like sacks of potatoes.
she's only 24 and already has
two or three kids by different dads;
she lost custody of them due to her
massive drug habit and her criminal record,
she's a well-known heroin addict
and lately she's been getting into GHB;
she'll even lecture you that GHB
is a natural substance that helps people,
and she thinks crystal meth
is a cheer-up party favor.
she sees pot as a comedown smoke
from all the H or the blow she does;
she's on reds to get to sleep
and does a line to wake her ass up;
she doesn't have a penny to her name
but that never stopped her from
having a good time out with the boys,
she's such a fun time they
always buy her drinks all night
and most offer to take her home to
do more drugs and drink more liquor.
she doesn't always come home,
she goes where the wind blows her.

told me she might move to Memphis
because here she's got nothing going on;
she doesn't count six months of us dating
as anything significant.
in fact, she and I are nothing at all, it seems

the mother moon sits heavy on me –
guarding me away from lunatic whispers,
the black of night eases me
allows me to sigh with genuine release,
the silvery light spraying everywhere
keeps the snarling wolves at bay;
a perimeter is implied by this moon –
a boundary is established by it,
a protective barricade is erected,
all foul thoughts will be squelched.
there will be only the happy people,
row after row of happy people
with monstrous, shining smiles
full of overly-white sets of false teeth;
people all singing in unison
like a mad musical come to life;
all perfect people allowed –
only perfect people allowed –
everyone else…get lost.
because today we are looking at
mass quantities of hope,
if only everyone could get
with the program and start to
look like the shimmering, happy people,
don't worry be happy–
they seem to have these lines
burned into their brains.
to watch them dance is disconcerting,
their nearly exact moves, performed
with nearly exact execution,
all at once – leave me breathless.
these people are like a million computer-controlled
marionettes moving in creepy, perfect synchronicity

"I think I'm falling in love with you,"
I said to her as I drove her home.
"Oh…that's not good… that's --"
"I know. It's bad. I told you
I had something terrible to say,"
I said, completely smothering
whatever she was trying to get out.
"I don't know what I was thinking,"
I continued.
There was total silence for the
rest of our long ride home.
When we got to her place
she hopped out quickly,
gave a strange look my way
and waved to me slowly.
And I never heard from her again.

I can't figure out what you want
from me - what you need,
you smile too often and talk too little;
we've been going out for months
and you have become more affectionate
but you have yet to even kiss me.
I don't want to spit on old fashioned ideas
but four fucking months?
you say you don't want to define us,
you want it to remain spontaneous;
well I'm seeing that's great for you!
all of the things you want, you get.
and somehow you have made no
commitment to me;
you've got me ready to buy you diamond earrings
and yet it seems you might disappear on some
new adventure or love any moment now…

Did you think I couldn't do it?
Think I couldn't pull the plug on us?
I asked you over and over
in so many ways to give me an answer.
But I came to see I would never
get from you any romantic response.
Months and months of going out
without so much as a kiss.
If I hadn't loved you so wholly,
as deeply as I did,
I can't imagine I would ever
have gone to such lengths over you;
I was certain you felt as I did
but that you were just slow to emotion - shy.
It struck me as quaint - charming.
But when I saw you
            with him
talking to him
asking so many questions about him
asking so many questions about him,
smiling that smile
                    at him
            it all hit home suddenly.
And I remembered, like a victim
in a bad horror film,
that you once were talking
to your girlfriend and you both
giggled because she had met a boy
she liked a week before
and had gone out on their third date.
You asked her, "Did you kiss him?"
and she nodded the affirmative.
Both of you laughed again
but the moment stayed with me.
When you like someone, you kiss them

you don't wait for some special moment to appear.
I totally misread you and I think you never
looked beyond my cover.

The bank manager called again
to say I went over by $350 again.
I apologized and sent a check
from another account but
I was actually cringing.
That's how bad things have gotten.
I can't afford a bed for
my new apartment.
I can't afford a TV yet.
Who the fuck doesn't have a bed
or a TV set?
Things are on a downward trend financially.
I've got nothing left on
my over-extended credit line.
I can barely afford the food
I'm eating and the gas to drive.
Everyone's freaking out about Iraq
but I'm freaking out about here.
There are major problems hitting us.
I'm not certain I can afford next
month's rent at this new place.
So it feels foolish buying a bed
when probably that money should
be set aside for rent.
To be sure.
It's terrible as yet another
holiday season rolls in
and again it appears I won't
be able to buy anyone
any-fucking-thing.

I pulled my Toyota sedan into a mini-mall
parking lot and went to a small diner
that was in the same building with
a 20+ lane bowling alley full of kids.
I noticed the "B" rating health
officials had stuck in their window.
It looked like a 50's Americana diner
but was known locally as a breakfast spot.
It was 6:15 pm; I had just woken up
so I'd headed over for eggs and such.
The chubby Mexican waiter came over
and I ordered chorizo and eggs
with a side order of French toast.
I washed it all down with o.j.
Then I went to the park and opened
up my laptop so I could get to work.

He ran screaming for his boy
through the streets of Baghdad.
But deep down he knew he'd never
hear his son respond.
Not after the last bomb dropped.
It was too close to the house
where he'd been staying with his aunt.
So he ran, for madness' sake,
screaming out his son's name.
U.S. soldiers got nervous about him,
since his movements were erratic
and he was screaming and pounding
his fists into his chest.
He threw a brick through a window
of a home supplies store.
One of the 19-year-olds from Cleveland
wasn't taking any chances—so he wasted
the tormented man.
The street was quiet then.
Or at least quieter.

What was I supposed to do?
She's hot but wants my money
so I broke up with her.
Little did I know she wouldn't
take it well.
She stole my car, burned my house
half down and got me fired
at the insurance agency where
I'd worked for over 17 years.
I'm married and was sleeping with
this other girl but I was lying.
The office girl didn't know
about my wife or two girls.
So she began to fantasize a life
that maybe we could lead together.
What started out as trips to Hawaii
and the Bahamas quickly turned
to discussions of how and when
we could move in together.
She got so lovey…so cuddly
when she talked like this
that I couldn't bring myself
to stop her dreaming.
Hell, I got caught up in the dreams.
They sounded nice.
But it got all too far along
and so I broke it off
and never told her why…not the truth anyways.

I rented an ultra-hip apartment in Hollywood
(on fucking Hollywood Boulevard too)
with a good d.j. friend of mine,
who was slinging blow on the side;
me and this guy we're still friends to this day,
but man, back then, two blocks off Fairfax near
the heart of the Strip we had THE PLACE.
the two-bedroom was huge, was super-cool,
with 1600 square feet, a mega-balcony
and plush carpeting so nice
it needed to be cleaned by a
special company using some patented technique.
we moved in on October 1, but
my roommate really moved in then.
I actually wasn't going to be ready to move
until December but I had
laid down cash and rent
to hold the pad.
me and this guy got along like you'd never believe,
I mean, there was no room we couldn't
take over, bowl over, own and bury.
this Hollywood spot was where I wanted to live.
and my buddy was with whom I wanted to live.
everything was perfectly fine,
if perhaps a little odd,
with me living there so part time
that my bedroom was empty for nearly six months -
not even a proper bed inside it,
just a mattress, a stereo and a bong.
I was still living part-time at my beach house
and times were fatter than I've ever had them.
this was a place no one could resist.
but I really wasn't there a whole hell of a lot,
I'd come through when Hollyweird had a job for me –
I'd come in for a three week shoot, party like

Keith Richards' evil twin brother –
SERIOUSLY -
then roll back to the beach or up to Monterey
where my family live.
I shoulda known from that first month though
that the apartment was a demonic doorway to
another dimension of lascivious bacchanals.
I mean, we laid our deposit down that first October
but then in late that same month,
before any of the Devil's work began
in earnest, I got
a phone call from the building's owner,
she told me she was calling to
alert me that we were close
to being evicted.
"evicted?" I asked, surprised.
"yes..we got another complaint
last night from three of your neighbors.
they heard loud music until 2 AM
and heard people talking and laughing
on the balcony until 3 AM.
"I wasn't…there last night."
"well, your roommate is causing a
lot of trouble over there."
"really?"
"really. he's into the party lifestyle
and I told you at the beginning,
we have lots of elderly tenants in
this building. having people over
for dinner is one thing. but
regular loud parties going until
3 and 4 AM is not going to fly around here,"
she was getting indignant.
it was true also that one of our neighbors
was one of the old, retired actresses from
"The Golden Girls" TV show.
"I'm sorry… I'll talk to him."
"I know you're not responsible but
if we evict you, and one more noise
complaint will do it, it goes on your record

for two years! your name is on the lease."
poor old bitches had no idea
that the P.O.D. (that's Prince of Darkness for
you newbie goodie-goodie assholes out there
trying to figure out what the fuck
any of this book is about)
and his best friend had moved into
the corner flat and that even our quietest,
most relaxed timeout was full of fucking,
drugging, drinking, screaming, singing,
art creation, music recording, orgies,
wrestling, upside down cross-type shit and so on and so on…

He was a doctor before a lawyer
and though hyper-educated he still
liked nothing more than a beer
and a couch with Sunday morning football.
So when his BMW 700 series was given
to him by his firm, he gave it
promptly to a charity benefitting children
whose families were killed on 9/11.
He didn't want ever to put energy
to negative causes so he worked
on meditation as a lifestyle.
He wanted to constantly be in
a meditative style of absolute centered calm.
So before his case was called in the courtroom
where he'd been trained to slay all comers,
I knew that in that fake bullshit room
where the biggest liars and cheats in the world
make their living by being "impartial" (a non-existent thing)
he'd seen through the veil of our society
and its "hallowed" foundations.
Everyone screamed, cried and shivered
when they heard the news –
the tragic, awful news -
but not me.
Not me.
I smiled when I heard and I laughed (with him!) -
when I went to a bar by myself and did a shot
of tequila to him – in his honor –
because he was braver than me or the rest of us
when he went to that court's bathroom and shot his brains out.

…betrayed by the nervous indignation on her face.
She was sweating, I think.
It seemed like she was sweating.
Her face was oily, moist -
she was serving me home mortgage papers
but didn't seem like she really wanted to.
She'd asked my name, I'd confirmed
and then she'd been standing before me
fidgeting with the envelope in her hand.
A minute or two passed before
she giggled and tried to clear her throat.
I wasn't giving her an inch.
Not a goddamn millimeter.
She'd have to do it.
Why not let her do her job?
So I stood in my doorway
just relishing her growing anguish
and palpably increased heart rate.
I committed myself.
I wasn't going to say a word.
No help. None. Tough love!
I didn't know if she was
a subpoena server by trade
or just by accident but the
latter category gained favor by my account.
She looked like she was peeing her
panties right on my porch, the
way her face contorted around.
Then I saw the puddle at her feet - she was pissing.
So I stepped back in total disgust.
I couldn't believe that shit!
On my damn porch.
What a thoughtless, crazy weirdo.
But I suppose the cocked .44 in
my hand had some contributing effect.

I'm starting to work at the lumber yard
because they are the only ones hiring.
They foreclosed my family house
and I've been drinking so bad I
can't seem to hold down an office job now.
I became worthless it appears.
They actually don't even want me at the
lumber yard, not really.
I just know one of the managers
back from when we were in 8th grade.
He must be looking at me with pity
pouring from his eyes.
But I wouldn't know.
I haven't been meeting a lot
of people's eyes lately.

They say I am a drunk
and so they have to do my
thinking for me.
I haven't had _that_ much to drink.
But maybe they know something.
Maybe they are the wise ones.
Maybe I will end up alone
and in a hospital by own hand.
But I don't feel crazy.
That is for sure.
I feel more subdued than ever.
In fact, I'm so weak and immobile
emotionally that I'm not even
capable of being a threat to myself.

…deal that coke before they see
what silly rooster clowns you
associate your silly self with.
No one could predict
the paths opening up so clearly
before such weary walkers.
And no one could foretell
the wraths glowing with such a
strong, unstoppable energy.
Wake them up and bake them up
if you want to dance in the
Cultural Riviera gracelessly sitting
down before the important people.

…and it's a lie that we are all one,
in the same boat negotiating the
same river, balancing the same weights.
Tricky, lucky drug dealers
flipping their junk just to get high
give real insight into the vicious cycle.
Sherlock it and you'll surmise
that we want to ignore the real hurt.
We want to look away but what
is scary is that if you thought
you could get away and say these
are crazy rants from a schizo,
you couldn't be more wrong.
You can't look away from what I
am showing you here; you can't.
That is because you know
in your heart of hearts that we
all look away because we'd fall
to our knees and fall to pieces if
we had to look, unprepared,
unsteadied, undrugged, undefended.
"Everybody can be somebody!"
"You can do it if you just believe!"
"America is a place of opportunity!"
"The land of opportunity!"
"Opportunity knocks!"
"Every tool you need to succeed
is available here in California!"
The man at midnight mass who
reeks of urine and worse, praying
in a church full of unnerved
parishioners not prepared for a
special show in Latin with organ
but presented in homeless smell-o-vision.
Pretty ladies splashing perfume

for their reeks, in the pews,
trying not to puke from the peeyew!
And the cold, harsh wind is outside,
flapping about, trying to ravage
everything living as if it derived
some twisted, natural order thrill from it.
The elements are unfeeling
and unconcerned with troubles of
the flesh so it's ironic that the
flesh shares those traits with the elements.
Emotional cannibalism is hard to
look at with eyes wide open,
sharks feeding on sharks calmly;
androids unplugging each other, excitedly.
When the police roll up, you
don't experience what I do,
what people like me do.
When cops rough you up before puberty,
it's bound to have some effect.
Hopelessness makes for inconvenient
company when role models
are in such short supply.
Can children really be crying
in the street tonight?
Only a few city blocks away…?
Can that be what it is?
What we get…?
Fucked up nightmares full of
multi-faceted psychoses swirling
around and blending like a horror smoothie
would be better than the cold,
cold realization that it is that simple.
That it is that rough and choppy
makes my heart pound and my throat dry.
I'm out in the cold
with a bunch of stupid Mexicans
just staring disrespect down
with a steely gaze that gets
me unsettled and fuels some wild-eyed,
aggressive behavior when confronted.

So I'm going to ask you just
one more time, asshole,
What the fuck did you say to me?

…by another night: without my son.
I am more of a failure
as a father than I ever could
have imagined was possible.
My son, my amazing, brilliant
little beautiful man is living
with his mother in a city far from me.
I have been shut out by her
in many ways because I have
made so little money as a stupid writer.
I am going to be dying again tonight
without him in my arms
or at least having seen him today.
I have to move to that city
or else move her here.
But moving her would take money
that I don't seem to have,
though I am in some disbelief about that.
I have made people lots of money
as a writer and yet, I don't have
enough money to care for my boy?
How can the money be flowing but
yet none goes to me?
Just a stupid, fucking writer.
And a pretty shitty one at that.
Where's the complexity of emotional
issues and where's the depth of
human spirit reflected?
I have been a hack
for so long, I may have
forgotten some of my natural instincts.
I have been so poor so long
that I can't remember when I
sold my soul to just get paid
enough to eat and have a roof.

I don't know if poverty
is what I experienced
but I also never had a
sense of savings, or of investments
or career-planning or job placement.
These were things I was aware of
but they were over there. Not here.
I have always and only ever
had one gift that others
seem to get some value out of:
telling stories about people.
So now I am more broke than ever,
with no credit cards, no drivers license,
no woman, no car and $15 in my pocket.
People want to know why
they haven't seen me in a while.
It's because I'm too broke to
do anything at all.
Coffee sounds expensive. For real.
And with my ex-wife scared
and raising my boy alone I find
I need to be with my son.
But a new city really scares me
very deeply because I won't
know anyone at all.
and in my life,
it has been the people I know
that have helped me, been there
and generally allowed me to
have some degree of certainty
as to my future.
I will have to be under the tough thumb
of my ex-wife who is a good woman
but sees me as the excuse
for all of her life's woes.
I don't care anymore.
Things like that, like my dignity,
were lost a long time ago.
I know I am the one who lost it.
I just don't remember when.

he was cleaning a toilet
when he broke down
and simply cried.
no one was around
and he let it out quickly
but he simply
couldn't hold it in,
not any longer.
he was shocked
as he kept realizing
just how far he'd fallen.
he was a prominent professor
at a major university
only a few years ago
but now
the only way he
could make ends meet,
since he'd lost the big job
was as a glorified janitor.
he was figuring out
he'd be managing an office
but his first
humbling day, on the job
gotten for him by a friend,
was all about finding out
that he was the attendant
at a business center.
he just needed to sit
behind a desk
point people to the bathroom
and occasionally fix that bathroom.
the drink and drugs,
had gotten him kicked out
of his old life
and the price was

certainly being paid.
he had almost walked out
when the manager
of the building handed him
a new broom
and pointed to an enormous
floor space.
but he stuck it out,
swept up,
said his "yes sirs"
and "no sirs"
and kept to himself.
a bag lunch
with a bologna sandwich
on white bread
and potato chips
was his staple
and he tried to keep away
from other people now.
he got a great distaste
for people now.
he'd soured on them
lost some faith perhaps.
anyway, he kept a distance
from any co-workers
and from the manager,
who was a smallish man
who also
hated himself totally.
before long
they were best of friends
and were drinking
and doing drugs
and scamming drug tests at work
together.
they'd watch the Lakers
and the Clippers on TV
or maybe go
pick up a hooker
at the "hooker hotel"

on La Cienega.
they would sit up
all night,
and just bitch
and play cards and chess.
they were both
very big on chess.
or maybe it was a new
game, drunken chess
since they never
played the game
any other way.
nothing could separate
the two
and even on the job
they sat side-by-side
eventually
giggling to one another,
talking shit under their breath
about all the stiffs
coming through the
big glass front doors.

DOWN THE HIGHLANDS WAY

The storm had raged for much longer than expected with no relent predicted. It was a rainy month but this particular downpour had found a mean wind as an accomplice and together they wreaked genuine havoc. Monterey isn't particularly known for being a place of harsh winters. In fact, it's fair to say that the town is widely considered to be at the center of the California coastline's most temperate climate zone. The twisting oaks and the lean, towering pines swayed roughly, morning and night under the constant assault.

Roberto Pérez couldn't keep his rickety rain gutters clear, so water would pool around the 59 year-old's house in odd ways. It kept finding its way under one of his garage doors. This irritated the trim, dark-skinned Chicano man who carried only the slightest hints of grey at his temples.

He was up on a ladder pushing leaves and pine nettles out of a particularly glutted gutter one morning when the rain let up momentarily. His pretty wife, Marta, came out the front door.

"Do you want papitas with your eggs or you want tortillas cut up into your eggs?" she asked.

"Whatever's easier," he replied, barely looking down.

"Cut up tortillas it is," she smiled.

"Thanks, sweetie."

"Hey, it's already six. Your coffee's cold and you're going to be late."

"Oh shit! Six? I'm coming right now," he smiled back. He looked up at the heavy rain clouds and got out as much blackening tree debris as he could before throwing in the towel and slowly climbing down the ladder.

Ana, 17, with long chestnut hair and Robbie Junior, 15, were eating waffles, eggs and sausage when Roberto entered the kitchen. Marta refilled the children's glasses of orange juice and took away empty plates of toast.

"Your plate's all ready...over by the micro," she said as she bustled about, putting dirty dishes into the sink.

"Thanks," Roberto smiled and grabbed his steaming plate of Mexican-style eggs and sausage. He sat with the kids.

"It rained so hard last night I thought my window was going to blow in," Robbie said, mouth full of breakfast.

"Is it ever going to end?" Ana asked.

"Paper says not until Thursday," Roberto answered as Marta brought him his cup of coffee.

"If it keeps up like this and the power goes out again…maybe they'll cancel school today," Robbie giggled. "In fact, maybe I'd better just stay home because it's probably going to happen, especially if it picks up again like it did yesterday."

"You're going to school, Robbie," his mother said as she walked off and towards the hallway leading to the bedrooms.

"I'm just saying, it's likely to happen, if you ask me. The teachers were getting ready to send us home but that damned power came back on. PG&E is pretty serious about this whole keep-the-lights-on thing."

"Get dressed," Roberto said, noticing Robbie had cleared his plate.

Robbie got up and trudged out of the kitchen and towards the bedrooms.

"How's Chem going, baby?" Roberto asked his beautiful, fully dressed and made-up girl.

"Awful. I hate it. Mr. Preston is mean and weird."

"That's every Chemistry teacher, sweetie. Did you get the grades from last week's quiz?"

"Yeah. Total b.s., Dad," she groaned, reached into her backpack, pulled out the quiz and handed it to her father.

"It's a B+. That's okay," Roberto said.

"It's b.s. Total b.s. He didn't cover chapters five or six at all in class."

"You'll make it up on this next quiz."

"Stanford's acceptance is still conditional on this semester's grades, remember, Dad?" she asked with some exasperation.

"You'll get 'em. You're beautiful, smart and dedicated. They're lucky to get you," Roberto said then gulped his coffee down.

"Aw, Dad…" Ana smiled then, leaned in and hugged him tightly. Then she got up and headed to a restroom.

Roberto was at the table alone. He gave his upcoming day a moment's consideration and chuckled. He put his coffee cup down and took a deep breath. The smile on his face slowly went away. He sat in silence, looking off into his own thoughts.

It really all started with the woodpeckers, the bad feeling that eventually crept over everything and made it into what it became. That evening as they ate a broiled chicken and steamed broccoli dinner, the storm came back full force.

"It's really coming down," Ana said.

"Yeah, and the wind is pretty crazy out there, Dad," Robbie added. Marta's chicken was one of their favorites so the four were enjoying every bite.

Suddenly – BAM – there was a massive thud on the roof that made Ana jump.

"Just a branch," Roberto reassured his daughter.

"The streets were full of branches," Robbie said, "I mean, the bus had to veer this way and that to get to my stop."

"The trees are swaying in a really scary way," Marta added.

"We should be okay but I noticed the same thing," Roberto replied. Their house was a lovely two-story that was Roberto's pride half because of the actual structure and half because of where it was. Roberto had been smart, lucky and hard-working and had bought into a great neighborhood in the late 70's when a strange drop in real estate prices allowed a middle-class guy like him to buy in. The whole Monterey area was rich with natural beauty but their neighborhood was particularly wooded. Tall pines surrounded the houses on their block and indeed were swaying and creaking more than anyone could recall they'd ever done.

The pines were mostly dotted with holes bored by a vibrant population of woodpeckers whose black and white feathers were accentuated by bright red ones. The holes were filled with acorns from the nearly equally numerous oak trees of the area. Now these pines were taller than one would expect. They were so long, stretching up to the sky, that if a person were to stand at the base and look up, even the heartiest of stomachs would give way to some symptoms of vertigo.

"Listen," Ana whisper-spoke.

And when they quieted for a moment, they could all hear the music of the pines creaking outside.

The fat clouds hidden by the gathering winter dark opened up and let loose just then with all their fury. Roberto's house was attacked by rain. It came from above and with the aid of the wind, from the side too.

And the trees hurled thin branches weighed down by heavy, green bunches of pinecones.

The lights flickered on and off but stayed on.

"Better get the candles and the flashlights," Marta said.

"I'll find the camping lantern," Roberto gave back as he stood and headed out to the garage. When he stepped outside he was pelted by the downpour.

"Dad's always got an answer," Ana smiled. Marta's smile back was tinted with thoughts held back and hidden.

The night was long and morning couldn't come quickly enough. When they were all up and looking out the front window they saw a yard and street filled with branches, bark, moss, pine cones and a whole general mess.

The City Road Service pulled up in the afternoon and had a chat with Roberto. After he came back in he said to the group, "They have to take down the big one…right outside Robbie's room. They said it's a miracle it didn't come down onto the house."

They went out the back sliding glass door through Robbie's bedroom and took a look. Sure enough, the fattest pine of them all had cracked in a frightening way. The bulk of its length dangled and swayed towards the house in a decidedly menacing manner.

The next day, with a lighter rain coming down, a city tree cutter truck showed up and the buzz saws could be heard echoing the grove all day. Yellow hard hats and cranes and ropes and pulleys were all given their fair chore in the serious task. Piece-by-piece those tough, cigarette smoking workers cut that big tree down to nothing but a stump. One hell of a big-ass stump.

"You gotta hire stump removers if you want that taken," the lead workman pointed to the four-foot wide remainder of what was once a magnificent pine rooted into the earth. They left the majority of the cut tree piled neatly beside the backyard fence since the monument had been taken apart and down in three foot increments.

Roberto examined the job and was initially impressed. It must have been some hard work to get that monster cut down to nothing but a stump. That much was clear to him. He was grateful that his beloved home was spared any possible damage from a falling pine as had happened to several others in the neighborhood over the 37 years he'd been domiciled there.

Like so many men who had come from nothing and worked every day for a lifetime, this house was his pride, second only to his daughter and son. But the house he took a particular personal pride in as he attributed much of his children's magnificence to his equally hard working and wise wife. So when he saw the big tree that wanted to smash his house in, broken down into neat piled pieces, he smiled. It was some relief.

But the strangeness began the very next day. It was Robbie Jr. who was first to notice it. He was sitting at his desktop computer squandering time online when something smashed into the window in the room he was in. He was sure some kid had thrown a baseball or a pinecone over the fence and it had hit the window, so he ignored it, but about ten minutes later it happened again.

He didn't see the object that had hit the window the second time either so he went outside into the backyard to look for the suspect ball or cone or whatever it must have been. But he couldn't find anything on the ground near the window that had been hit twice with such force he couldn't believe the glass hadn't broken. He really looked around too. But there was nothing there.

He logged off the computer, went into the living room and turned on the television to watch some sports journalists arguing over the year's top contenders to make the Superbowl. He got a slice of pizza, microwaved it and sat back down on the big black leather couch. Not ten minutes passed before the window next to him was hit just as hard as the one in the other room had been. But this time, Robbie looked up in time to see the culprit: a woodpecker.

He went outside again but this time looked up into the trees. Sure enough, on the branches of a much smaller pine than the one that had been chopped down, were perched four or five woodpeckers.

"Stupid fucker," Robbie said in pity for the bird that must have run straight into the window at full force. He didn't think about it until the next day when it happened four more times.

With the whole family eating hamburgers and corn the fourth hit to a window drew Robbie outside.

"What are you doing?" Marta asked her son.

"These woodpeckers are attacking the house. I swear, they mean to do it."

"Nah…it's got to be they're just confused," Roberto said.

"No. No. This is the second day and they just keep hitting the windows at their hardest," Robbie refuted as he came back in the house and sat back down to his food.

Ana laughed, "They're after you, Robbie!"

"No. It's the tree. The big one. That got cut down. It was their home or something. And they're pissed," Robbie theorized.

They finished their dinner but before the night was through, two more hits came to different windows by the birds. No one said anything. But it didn't go unnoticed.

The woodpeckers started up again the next morning and their assault was more ferocious than before. They were undoubtedly smashing themselves into the house with violent energy sometimes two or three times in a row. And when they didn't fly beak-first into a window, they'd land on the house and peck at it, making holes in it until it drove Robbie and Roberto to run out and holler them off.

But, if anything, the attacks were increasing and aggravated by the boys' angry responses. The woodpeckers seemed to congregate on the two pines that were closest to the big one that had been felled.

Roberto was out watering the plants in the backyard the next day when he saw that the woodpeckers were again gathered as if in wait. He picked up a pinecone and threw it at them with some accuracy. It scattered them but they really only flew a few feet and re-landed on the nearest branches of pines or oaks on the property.

And the incidents of birds smashing into the house increased in frequency. It was hard to not feel an anger from the birds in the way they'd fly right into the house windows over and over. Even the neighbor made a comment to that effect to Roberto when he also had witnessed the odd avian behavior.

Even when the storm front had moved on and blue skies returned the birds continued their siege on the house. Their anger seemed undiminished by the days and even weeks that passed.

Just as Robbie Jr. had been the one to first notice the strange woodpecker activity he was also the one to first notice something strange about his father.

He was sharp for one so young and an inconsistency in Roberto's daily patterns brought him to find things hidden in his father's bedroom closet.

Every day Roberto would head off to work at the educational materials publishing company he'd worked at for over 35 years at the same time: six am on the dot. And each night, Roberto would stay in his room doing his work for the next day. He'd be editing this new teacher's edition of a Spanish Two textbook or that edition of a middle school U.S. History textbook. But it was Robbie who noticed, one evening passing his father's desk of work, that the date on the materials was a year old.

So the next night, he made an excuse to pass by his father's desk again and found that the work on the desk was the same as the night before. Not similar or a different version of the work…but the exact same pages. Checking Roberto's desk nightly now became Robbie's mission. And sure enough, every night, Roberto's pages of work were the same ones that were always there. Day after day, Roberto was pretending to do work. Ana, with her tattooed rocker boyfriend, didn't notice. Marta, with her part-time clothing store clerk job and household duties with the children's homework, didn't notice.

Finally, Robbie got bold enough to make a confirming move. He called to his father's office and putting on a deep, disguised voice, he asked the company operator for his father's extension. She said what Robbie probably already knew: no such extension existed.

This troubled Robbie but he wasn't sure what to do about what he'd discovered. Where did his father go every day? And what did those endless shoe boxes filling his closet contain?

A few weeks later, when his parents were away for an overnight trip to visit an ailing relative and Ana had gone to the movies with her boyfriend, Robbie took the opportunity to open the shoe boxes. They were full of business envelopes addressed to Roberto Sr. from the bank.

Robbie opened all the shoe boxes and each one had the same thing inside. Envelope after envelope of bad news from their bank about the mortgage on the house. The high-schooler couldn't follow all the language nor its meaning but the general gist was plain enough: they were in trouble with the house. Payments had been missed. Legal proceedings had begun. Refinancing had been rejected and so on and so on.

Roberto had been fired and had probably been losing the house for some time but had kept it to himself. Robbie felt lied to for a moment. What a farce, he thought to himself. Robbie's anger was the first of his emotions to surface.

Through a network of young friends, Robbie found out that his father had been working at a coffee shop in nearby Salinas just to keep some money flowing into the family's bank account; just to keep food on the table. When one of these buddies covertly uncovered his father's real job, Robbie was at once overcome with a sense of guilt at having only the week prior insulted his father for being "too cheap" to buy him the latest X-Box 360 video game. Robbie shook his head at himself…a goddamned video game. He felt small. Very, very small. But then, being of the same moral and character stock as his father, he felt something else he'd never ever taken the time to internalize in his life: he felt a swelling pride at the heroic, quiet strength of the man who had given him everything; the man who never complained and never bought a thing for himself. Robbie felt suddenly very big. Very, very big.

So when the events that followed took place, Robbie always kept his knowledge to himself but he harbored an odd, newfound respect for his old man. One that he kept with him until he himself was an old man many decades later with children of his own.

Roberto went to the house of his longtime and unmarried best friend, Gregorio (Greg), on a warm Spring night soon after and sat for tea with him. Tea was Greg's style. The two talked football and basketball, as they loved to do, but Greg could tell that something was different this night; something betrayed by the subtle, nearly imperceptible shifting redness passing across Roberto's cheeks. Greg began to get a strong feeling of worry that coursed his veins until he could not hold back any longer.

"What is going on, Roberto? You always come over on Sundays but here you are on a Wednesday night," Greg inquired nervously.

Roberto's deep piercing eyes gave no comfort and his silence even less.

"Roberto…?"

There was a long pause. "Yes?"

"I asked you if you're okay? What's going on?"

"Nothing. Everything," Roberto intoned eerily.

"Are you okay?"

Another long pause. "The woodpeckers showed me," Roberto said.

"Showed you what?"

"What I should feel. What…I should do…"

"You're really freaking me out, Roberto. I don't understand," Greg said.

Roberto reached into his coat and pulled out something. Greg's eyes moved over that hand with a twitch. Then Roberto placed seven or eight pages of computer printout pages on the table between the two men. Greg looked at the papers with nothing short of crystal clear guilt.

"What are these?" Greg asked with hollowness.

"Go ahead. Read." After a tense moment then, "It's okay," Roberto said quietly.

Greg took the white sheets, unfolded them and began to take in what was printed on them. It didn't take him but a moment to put the pages down along with his eyes and along with his head.

"Roberto…I—I don't know what to—to----I'm so…" he stammered on.

Roberto chuckled to himself curtly. His eyes too were on the floor. "I've known for some time," Roberto said.

Greg began to cry.

"Apparently she loves you too. These e-mails are not…unclear," Roberto said.

"I'm scum. I--I don't know what possessed me. You're my best friend and I… do this to you…"

"Marta and I have not slept in the same bed for almost six years now. But I think you know that."

"Oh God…Roberto…"

Roberto then reached into his pants pocket and pulled out a gun.

Greg nearly fell backwards out of his chair, eyes wide with utter fear as he stared at the gun in his friend's hand.

"Are you going to shoot me?" Greg whispered.

After a long, uncomfortable moment of silence, Roberto replied, "Actually, you're going to shoot me."

Two weeks later they went together down to Big Sur for a supposed fishing trip (something that was rather common for the two, to go past Carmel and past the Highlands and right past Pfieffer State Park) and after setting up camp, they walked deep into the woods. They had on hiking gear and all the accouterments of men heading to a fishing hole for the day.

Roberto explained, "You two have been in love for over six years. She really loves you and plans to leave me for you as soon as Robbie goes to college in two years. I lost my job. I'm about to lose the house that is the only thing – the only material thing – I ever cared about. I've already lost my best friend. And I'm dead broke. I'm 59. No one is going to hire me. I'm going to watch my children go off and then be in the way of what I can tell is a real love between you and my wife. I have nothing. I'm a forty five year-long cigarette smoker. I've seen no doctors, but you've heard the rattle of my cough. We both know what my lungs must look like. And now, Ana, my dear Ana, has gotten into Stanford pre-med. Fifty thousand a year. And with the economy and the cutbacks on grants and scholarships…she's not getting anywhere on that road without hundreds of thousands of dollars. But I found a loophole. A loophole in my life, if you will, Greg. Three years ago, just before the crash of '08, you remember the company was about to make me a partner. Well… they took a life insurance policy out on me. To the tune of one million dollars. My children are all that matter to me now. And I don't want them to see a broken, hateful man whose wife cheated and left him. You're going to do me one last favor, to redeem your friendship to me. You're going to shoot me, make it look like a random homeless man shot and killed me for this fancy Rolex I'm wearing and then Marta and you will wait two years to reveal what you will make appear as a newfound love after my passing. And my children will get over the loss of their childhood home by going to the best colleges. They will remember me as a strong father who had a loving, devoted wife, their honorable mother, and they will get the educations that will take them where they belong in life. Do you understand me, Greg?"

"What if I say no?"

"I'll find someone else to do it. This is your job. Your punishment. And your redemption. To me."

Greg shivered as they walked the trail.

Then they arrived at the spot Roberto had chosen.

"You know what to do with the gun and how to tell the story of how you ran for your life after 'the man' shot me. How to deal with the police and with Marta. Now…go ahead. Let's do this," Roberto said as he turned around.

"I'm not sure…I'm…"

"Goddamn it, you asshole, DO IT NOW!!"

Greg lifted his shaky hand with the heavy gun in it.

And then he shot his best friend in the head, tears in his eyes.

That morning, before he'd left to go pick up Greg for their 'fishing-camping trip', Roberto had hugged Ana and Marta and Robbie Jr.

Robbie hugged him particularly tightly and for a long moment – not knowing exactly what was coming but knowing that something was off.

Marta flipped the pancakes and asked casually, totally unaware, about his and Greg's day, "Where you guys going to fish?"

As he got started closing the front door after him, Roberto smiled at Ana and Robbie warmly, "I'm just going down the Highlands way."

She loved Heavy Metal and it was 1997
and shit,
so she had like
all that memorabilia crud all over
the place - her room -
like posters of Ratt and Mötley Crüe
and Black Sabbath and Dio and Dokken.
I can't forget Dokken here.
She also had posters of Metallica and Iron Maiden,
AC/DC, Zeppelin, Warrant, Poison,
Danzig, Megadeth and, of course, Kiss.
She smoked pot with me
and her friends and we did
like
way too much acid,
but it wasn't harsh on
the stomach or anything
and it had strong visuals so
we just ate burritos
which was kinda like
-swimming in jello-
but that's not really
the best way,
probably,
to, like, describe it - the feeling
of tripping hard ass
while staring at posters of Ronnie James Dio
and Glenn Danzig and seeing them
come out of the posters and start to
sing and dance
but, like,
songs by Barney the Dinosaur-
"I love you, you love me."

she sold her sister out
for a few quarters of crank
and the thugs ended up
beating the woman brutally.
her sister deserved it,
she told herself while
taking out a credit card
to chop up the yellowish
powder which was now
in abundance.
her sister was a fool
for even getting such people
angry, she told herself
while rolling a dollar bill
up tightly.
her sister always pissed off
men and women too, she
told herself while pulling
her hair back, covering one
nostril and leaning down to
snort the fat rails.
her sister shouldn't have
ratted on these drug dealers
in the first place, she told
herself while leaning back
and dealing with the drips.
her sister was a fool for
not leaving town, she told
herself while drinking a
tall glass of water to
get that taste out of the
back of her throat.
her sister's face would look
normal in a few months,
she told herself while
opening a beer at 11 AM.

Reagan Babies in pretty pieces
sliced up and put in thick stew
for elven princes to eat
after shooting snuff films of
moralist, right-wing plagues
aborting swaths of multi-colored
euthanasia and welfare cock sucking,
dangled high shit from anus puckers
and priests of Dildo Majesty
with a Catholic background fueling
manipulation and carcinogenic
mindsets banked on with
Presidential authority covering
debts to brown peoples with
mouths sewn shut by
leather chains of steel,
liquid but immovable
and stretching across the
orders of child molesting monsters
who live in the armpit of limos
with whores for tires.
gutters of blood are nothing
to jackals with hunger
and to amusement park murderers
who have cartoon killers
at their fingertips.
Reagan Babies sucking dick
on the cross bleeding
static down to Nazi boots
echoing crimes across
a demented, decayed
landscape of burned out
fundamentalism
forced on the free

I want to kiss her cheeks
her neck
and run my hands
along her shoulders
as we sit on an empty beach
just looking at one another
touching one another.
I want to kiss that smile
that picks up my heart
and makes it alive again,
throbbing again with vitality.
I want to have her hair,
long and brown fall over my face
as she giggles and tickles me.
I want to wake up to
this face and watch her
all the time I can:
we were silent sometimes
for hours just kissing
and looking at each other in bed.
I loved to slap her ass
when I'd get up to pour wine
or to get a beer.
She'd always get faux-mad
and chase after me,
ready to wrestle,
and we usually did.
She was most sexy in her underwear,
teeth gritted, muscles flexed
trying to pin me down.
She's so hot, my lady
I could really overheat
just from smelling her perfume
or from the sway of her hips.

I was having 3-ways
with sexy fun ladies
before I ever published
a word professionally
or made a feature film.
So shut the hell up
with that noise about
using the arts to get laid.
I always loved getting laid,
I'm just making "art" now
and continuing being
who I am.
My girlfriends and I would
go pick up girls
and go home to have sex together
since long before I knew
I'd be involved with any of
this whole media crap.
I was a sick perverted
threat to your pretty little girls
since before any of
this L.A. gig.
So don't blame writing, or actresses,
or Hollywood or money
or any of that crap.
Blame me. Carlos.
Flat out, blame me.
I'd prefer it.

…and that smile of yours is a dead giveaway.
You are mad at me and will not forgive me.
In fact, that half-smile, here, in front of
all these party-goers is very scary to me.
You won't even make real eye contact with me.
I reach for your hand and you won't let me take it.
You look anywhere but in my direction.
And when you finally do see me,
you give me that fake smile that means
I've gone too far this time
and there'll be no coming back from this.
We are completely through.
This is what I see in that crooked smile.
The other guests, drinks in hands, think
we look like the perfect couple.
They have no idea that come morning
we won't be an item anymore.
They are confused by the icy attitude you display.
They don't know how much I've hurt you.
They just see another girl crying over some lost emotion.
I'm getting lots of dirty looks at this party.
You keep yourself busy, hoping no one
notices that you are changing rapidly inside.
But when I look at you,
really look into you,
that smile is backed up.
The smile that says We are through for good
is all you have to offer me now.

She sat angrily puffing at a cigarette,
wondering
where her good-for-nothing boyfriend
had gone off to
this time.
Was he fucking the little red-head
or was he doing heroin again?
It's not like he would
tell her
if he was cheating or using.
They had absolutely no trust
between them
to the point that neither
one really even
wanted
to try to make their
relationship
work
anymore.
Double your
pleasure
in the boxing ring.

Matt lost $80 in a poker game
but he smiled as he left the
house and went off to kill himself.
He even made plans for a hiking trip
to take place the following week,
but apparently he went
to his truck, drove a mile
or two and shot himself in
the head while going 95
on the freeway at night.
The bloody, fiery ball of
flames reached up into the
black sky dotted with
early-night stars.
Was it the $80 or was
it that he was still depressed
over the lost job or was
it the lost girl?
Maybe it was just the
$80; sometimes it's hard
to tell.

Dance
with
grace
of
heart's
desire
and
sky's
divine
horizon
love
song
eloquence
misanthropically
interpreted
from
low-rider
stereotypical
jeers
and
cheers
of
crowds
non-believers
and cheerleaders
both
waving
their
pom-poms.

Depravity is my calling card
when my blood gets hot enough
to actually make me go out to
seek female companionship.
Some cads start out with
a dashing exec routine
or a healthy hippy line
but my method also works.
Low-life, alcoholic, unshaven
beer-belly and a t-shirt
low-rent mindset fits me
like a tailored glove.
My prurient interests always
seem to get played out my way
when I am at my most
despicable and odorous.
Let's not overlook the smell
factor which truly plays
a large role in the "DEPRAVITY
SYSTEM" of attracting women.
"DUMB" is hipper than you
know and "SMELLY" is
finally coming into its own.

THE PENINSULA

...so, welcome
to the Peninsula. This is the home of the modern monarchs
and the unknown ones who live in Paradise.
Welcome!
To the Peninsula.
Where celebrities find peace
mingling with artisans and small-town quiet.
Welcome.
To the Peninsula,
home of the American golf zeitgeist
and throne of those who rule the world.
Welcome!
To the Peninsula.
Where rich natural beauty melts
into fertile soil that feeds a nation:
the edge of the world
where the surfline finds a stop,
a place to rest its weary shoulders
if only for the time of a breath;
the curl of a flamelick,
like Jason's ingenious ploy
to get a hold of the fleece;
it makes the chum thick here.
Torrential rain comes here only
every 30 years (or so) but on a cycle
borne out over endless waves
by an ancient insatiable energy.
Social mobility comes here only
every 30 years (or so) but on a cycle
borne out over endless loans
by a "pretty old" insatiable anger/fear –
(fear/anger being a singular concept
that needs a word. It is obvious

that fear/anger (fanger?) (fearnger?) is a
concept we as a species are not yet ready
to have a single word for. Or maybe it's just English.)
It is the sleepiest
of little sleepy towns
and no one quite can
enunciate the precise charm
it drapes over new eyes.
You are drawn in before you figure out
you've been glamoured.
You're walking on a beach
or through a forest
or through a great hall
when you first concede
you are hooked.
Done for.
Toasted on both sides.
But...
Welcome to the Peninsula.
Heart and soul of the murder
capital county of California (2009 & 2010).
Welcome
To the Peninsula,
where gang slayings in nearby
Salinas spill over – all over...
Welcome
To the Peninsula,
where high-end, quality drugs
of any kind are in abundant supply.
A quaint murder capital county town
with the CIA director hanging out
at church and Hells Angels
still sputtering up from down the coast.
A silly little collection of "cities"
near the sea trying to stay small;
it's a place of elegance and gaudiness;
the two intermingling so extensively
as to make them nearly indistinguishable
in the rarified airs of this place.
The old bags on Ocean Avenue

wear the most ridiculous,
horrible, multi-colored sweaters
that cost them a small fortune.
The Bentleys roll Forest Lodge Road
and Stevenson Road but make sure
to steer clear of Fremont's
bowling alley, Motel 6 and porn store
complete with jack-off booths.
Besides, the Bentleys have killer
in-car, hi-def screens and Blu-Ray players
so they can whack off
in their ride and maybe, just maybe,
pay their driver to watch them do it.
And what about the Grove?
The dirty, dirty Grove?!
with all the meth and Oxy
flowing through this shady wood
you'd think it was a
bizarre narcotics study being
conducted by watchful alien scientists.
Welcome
To the Peninsula.
Where there are more escort services
than sports fields for the kids,
the thing this place is supposedly
all about and shit.
Welcome
To the Peninsula.
With more charities than charity,
where animal rights supersede human rights,
and where lettuce pickers can
make people rich but can't
get a fair education for their children.
"Fun place to visit, though,"
says the fat guy in the Lamborghini
with a blond a third his age.

he ran through the office screaming
that he was the boss
and that changes were being
put into effect to bring about order.
two days earlier all his employees
had signed a letter to the owner
of the small company requesting
the manager's resignation.
the letter specified that
he was disorganized, emotionally
unstable, under-productive,
a constant yeller, into playing
mind games with employees,
often found berating a customer.
it went on and on crucifying him.
they'd had just about enough
of his bullshit and had banded together.
so now came his response
to finding out about their treachery.
he ran around the entire office
pulling down posters with positive affirmations
written on them and then he crumpled them.
then he ran around yelling,
accusing different employees of theft
and incompetence and other such lies.
then he started sending out memos.
each memo was angrier than the previous.
one said all computer video games
had to be deleted from all computers
in order to increase productivity.
another said, the color green
should be avoided in employee clothing
because it was the color of a competitor's logo.
another prohibited talk in the elevator.
they just got more and more nuts.

he was out on his ass so fast.
his big head is still spinning
six months after the fact.

She's got the saddest eyes
I've ever seen in this world
and it endears me to her
in a way I cannot figure out.
She's a pillar of her community
and a real natural beauty to boot.
She's got a walk
that you'd just love to see
if you have any man in you.
And her lips,
when they are close to you --
it's best to stay still
and hope they land on you.
She can tell the funniest joke
but I know what she's
really thinking deep inside.
Where she doesn't want
to let anyone into.
She thinks the whole world
is a pile of shit.
She thinks dreams are bullshit
and that no one in this life
gets anything close to
what they deserve.
She hides this fear away.
It's her big secret really.
She's a wife, a mom,
an upstanding moral woman
in an upstanding small town
but what she keeps locked up
is that she's not strong at all.
Everybody quivers around her,
snaps to her beck and call;
but my eyes are piercing
(if I have no other good qualities)

113

and she is simultaneously attracted to
and afraid of that.
She knows I know
and somehow that comforts her
even just a little.

blood sprayed all over them
with each man they shot
at such close range.
screaming could be heard
all across the valley
and then they ran into the woods,
across the river
and to the waiting car.
they hopped in it and didn't
hesitate to speed off
down the long winding highway.
after driving for a week
they were on a different coast,
and shacking it at a shit motel.
with the money they now had,
they'd go in bars at night
picking up roadside skanks
for bouts of casual sex.
they moved on soon after
and went to Mexico
for a good solid year
before migrating north again
and settling into Texas.
after what they'd done
and how many people'd seen it
they had no other option
but to live like this.
new city, new name, new life
every couple of months.
but with all the cash
they kept under the mattress
it didn't occur to them
to try to live
any other way.

he's throwing a pre-party party
at an art gallery in Venice.
he's invited all the hottest women
and a few local illuminati
to his hippy soiree.
he'll be selling bags of weed
and ecstasy and a few mushrooms.
I don't even know
what type of art
this gallery specializes in.
but based on Olev's parties
and his overall tastes it's probably surrealist
artwork that will be all over the walls.
I'm sitting here, smoking a joint
trying to figure out
what I want to do tonight.
my cute friend is seeing
another boy tonight
so getting laid is totally out.
the movies are offering little,
theatre in L.A. depresses me,
so this party is looking better.
I wouldn't mind meeting
a beautiful, pot-smoking woman
who happens to love nice art.
Olev knows how I get around his girls and so
I'm surprised he called to invite me.
he must be hoping
that I'll be on my best behavior.
I suppose that depends
on how many of his drugs I ingest.

he looked down
out of the huge helicopter
and saw the ground below
whizzing by like a videogame.
farms and houses and forests
were all blended in a blur.
he gripped his rifle tightly
in a strange moment of panic attack.
he'd never done a mission
of this magnitude before.
what could occur in a
foreign, hostile city
with his American ass
running around, gun in hand?
looking at his weapon
he wasn't sure if it would
end up saving him
or end up getting him killed.
it was the painted bull's-eye
on his carcass that
they'd later laugh about.
he wasn't totally sure
how he felt running through
this particular city at this
particular time with this
newbie squad from hell.
passing his eyes over the
other soldiers also tensely
awaiting their drop-off
he had the casual thought,
"what if we're all the
Special Forces' losers and the
idea is to get the bunch of us all killed
in one simple decoy mission
of no real significance?"

the Blackhawk slowed down
and the pilot started barking instructions.

She was the most beautiful Vegas showgirl
back in 1973, but now she's
just a 240 pound, acne-covered sow
with no manners, friends or style.
She's a pill-popping mother of seven.
Only three of her children still keep in touch
and two of them only because they
are under 18 and still live under her roof.
She's a street walker on weekends
or on holidays and the rest of the time,
she panhandles in downtown Vegas.
She's toothless but still has humor
and she uses it all the time to juice
just another dollar out of a geeky tourist.
The police know her on a first name basis
and so when she sees a patrol car
she'll hobble off into an alley way
or sometimes she'll duck into the movies.
She can't afford a ticket but she'll use
their bathroom and waste time pretending
to be looking over a movie show schedule
as if she plans to pick one any moment.
When the cops turn the corner,
she's out of the theater and back on the street
with her little white cup in her hand.
As tourists walk by she's joking
with them good-naturedly and eventually
they start to shell out quarters and dimes
for the pathetic soul before them,
and she'll hitchhike home then
and pull out canned soup to put on
for her kids, the two young ones.
Sure, she has no idea where they are
when she gets home but she knows that
just like stray cats, they'll come around
and when they do, they're always hungry.

You want to bomb some Muslims
and see them scatter in fear?
Want to clear out a continent
for an oversized hot dog stand?
I'd like to march a party train
across the ocean and onto land.
Stamp a big American flag on their asses,
whipping up a storm as we whiz by
in our Humvee limos and Rolls Royces.
I'd like to see waves rise up
in the sea and swallow Iraq up.
Perhaps the President would be happy
and perhaps New York children
could once again sleep without
having to listen to their parents sob
ever so-quietly all through the night.
I'd love to see a parade of show dogs
come down prancing from
the heavens above only to ravage us–
every last human on the planet.
They would be demonic hounds
sent by an angry deity tired of
listening to all of our debates about
the real sanctity of life and what all.
I could see the newspaper men
getting very excited at the prospect
of reporting on such supernatural happenings.
"These angel dogs seem to be devouring
whole city blocks of citizens. Now
back to you and Judy in the studio…"
I'm still unsure what good we can find
in the hearts of such awfully tired souls.
Do we dare to keep looking, with no promises
of what we are to find or not find?

I can't pay for the dinner I'm eating
so I will dine and ditch
when the ever-trusting waiter
turns his back for more than a minute.
I'm not usually a thief
but when my credit cards were
all shut off and my wallet dried
I found myself in a strange situation.
I decided after two nights of
being rained on outside
in a ratty little alley
that I was going to have to
make some very real changes.
I started with shoplifting food.
I'd pocket pre-made sandwiches
or cans of soup or bread from the deli.
My hands became super dexterous.
I knew cameras were in these stores
but you know what I've discovered
about all those endless miles
of security camera footage that
all those cameras generate, 24-7?
It's hard to know which section
of tape to really scrutinize
in order to catch a thief.
So, the more casual you act
as you commit the crime
the more likely you are to be uncaught.
When those manager-security types
look over those tapes,
believe me, all they see is an endless
parade of consumers grabbing
things off the shelves greedily.
They don't know who's paying for what,
so, I chose not to let myself starve.

Crawling so long makes you growl
even when the other dogs
are being totally calm—
you want to rip into them.
blood in my eyes, lips cracked
and you can stop looking down
on this shit you've overlooked.
I'm that shit you've dismissed.
I'm that shit you've left behind.
I'm that bullshit you call nothing.
I'm that shit. That's me.
But the funny thing about shit
is that a real nasty one
sticks to the bottom of your shoe
and you never get rid of it.
I'm that sewer scat you
could have sworn you flushed.
You've painted me in a corner
made a mockery of my name,
and insulted all of my people.
So when someone's been
pushed into the ground
and humiliated beyond
their own comprehension,
what type of reaction do you think
they'll give when they do
finally stand up and say,
"Enough."
I don't like to think
about nuclear-car-wreck-blasts
that fuck bodies up like that
personally.
But that's just me.

I filled the toilet with puke
and continued to do so
for a good six to eight hours.
Goddamn Thai shithole gave me
a serious case of food poisoning.
I was so weak and nauseous
I couldn't even get my ass
to a hospital or clinic.
Somewhere early in the nightmare
I made the decision to just
tough it out like a man.
I screamed, I cried, I died
in that bathroom.
And then I was resurrected.
I awoke with my face in puke.
I had no idea how long
I'd been there for.
I'd suffered an entire evening
of gut-wrenching pain
but I'd obviously passed out.
It had been too much
for my normally-iron stomach
to handle and that still surprised me.
I cleaned myself off,
drove to the Thai place,
waited until dark came
and when no one else saw
I capped the three cooks,
two assistants, a waiter
and one of the co-owners.
I felt bad later
for doing that
but not bad enough
to not stop off for donuts
on the way home.

She's semi-nude in a sexy bunny outfit
and she pulls down her top
to show me everything she's got.
I stick my face right in
and get to licking her tits.
My hand goes down the front
of her ultra-tiny short shorts.
We're kissing soon after and
between kisses she starts to
instruct the other party guests
on how to go find their own rooms.
She's had a few orgies
but tonight she wants one-on-one
with yours truly so she shoos
everybody upstairs and into back rooms.
We're fucking on the couch
before the room is empty.
Two of her girlfriends even come over
and watch the sexual proceedings.
Later, we're in a hot tub
kicking back with champagne
when she springs it on me.
She saw my last photo exhibit
and she's just getting started
at trying to be a serious model.
She's hoping I'll do a photo shoot
that she can be part of
or preferably do a shoot
all for her.
I tell her it's not like that.
I don't really plan shoots.
She promises that she'll provide
plenty of spontaneous moments
worthy of my attention.
The look in her eyes
makes me believe her.

No one wants him to return
and they're all doing their best
to send him subtle messages
to let him know just that.
Some called and told him
they'd be out of town for the holidays.
He knew they were lying.
Some are calling now and
doing quite a good fake.
They don't invite him over
during the holiday times
but they extend an invite
for a fishing trip in February.
He knows the fishing trip
will fall apart due to "weather"
and he knows that they know
this too as they offer it.
Some are coming up
with really creative excuses.
One of his friends now
has an aunt who's quite ill
with an odd lymphatic disorder.
Problem is, he knows the guy's aunt
died some five years earlier.
One friend claims he's so
mentally distraught these days
that he's entering a clinic
for the mentally-in-question.
This lie almost held up
until he ran into the
"mental case" at a cheesy bachelor party,
stuffing dollar bills into a g-string,
with his teeth as he whooped
and slapped the girl on the ass.

Dana, the man, the monster, the myth,
whips all around in his SUV
yammering on his cell phone
to screenwriters and actors around town.
While running errands for his boy
he gives out story notes.
"Yeah. Just change the main character
to a woman. And now the ending
can be different. Plus add a
different villain...hold on, I'm at
the deli...yes...get one pound
of the fresh roast beef, turkey...kill the
opening. Yes. I'm talking to you again.
The opening-- one pound. One pound.
And I need two pounds of roast beef.
The opening sucks. Hello. Hello. Yes.
We need something a little more amazing.
You've got to blow the audience away.
You've got to slice that up better.
Huh? No. Not you. I'm talking to the deli guy.
One pound of cheddar, sliced, please. Jesus.
Fucking Mexican help. No. I know
you're technically Mexican but you're
one of those Spanish kind. Not a Mexican.
Sure. Maybe you are 'Mexican' but
you're not gutter like these people.
So back to that miserable opening scene--
Wrap it up in plastic bags please.
Kill the love interest. Yeah. It's fair
to say we need a major rewrite.
I'd be fine with throwing the concept, the lead,
the villain, the theme and the dialogue out
and keeping the parts that are good.
Can I pay for this here? Oh. Up front.
Fine. Hey. I'll call you back, okay?"

pumping all types of shit
all over housing and children
while tearing at the sky's edge,
ripping a hole in the known.
stomping mountains of ideas
into a flat surface with little effort.
smiles beaming upon the moon
and eyelids torn up by nasty terrorists.
it's really a TV time,
a super-duper posh time-
a cracker jack, smack it up time.
you can't sit down for this shit.
it'd really be a crime to
miss the volcanic fireworks.
don't try to defend the smallness.
step on over to the bigness.
turn around and forget seasons
and their debilitating effects.
take the present as the
most important time
and try to leave room for dessert.
it's a non-fat, low-cal,
no-additive, no artificial color time.
so I think you'll be fine.
you're wearing jeans and waving
a big American flag so I'm not worried
the boat passing by is not sinking,
it only looks that way
from where you are watching it.
kick back and order a masseuse
up to your hotel room.
it's a room-service, mini-bar,
free cable, pay-per-view porno
kind of time so try not to worry so much.

he raped two women
before he was 27
and it didn't bother him any.
he'd gotten away with both
and was quite quietly proud of it.
he snickered when he saw
women by themselves
away from a crowd for a moment.
"you could be mine,"
he'd whisper aloud.
he was actually quite content
and figured to add a third rape
to his résumé before long.
he was just picking
his target and that took time.
he wasn't a spontaneous rapist.
he was a pre-planned
spidery-type rapist
lurking in shadows,
following his victims
for days to learn their routines
and the weaknesses within.
he'd wait until just
the right moment
and add one more notch.
he was so happy that he
was going to have a third victim
that before going out to hunt
he sat down to a pancake and eggs
breakfast at a 24-hour diner.
then he thought about the face
of his last victim,
walked outside to smoke
but instead blew his brains out
against a crappy pay phone.

he had a way of presenting things
so that when he was through talking
no one really knew what
he'd said but they knew they agreed with him.
he could spin stories all night long,
and that's still one of the most profitable
career choices around these days.
you'd think he was a lawyer
or perhaps a politician but no
he was simply a traveling man-
someone who'd seen so many adventures
that even when describing small events
he could entrance a hall full of listeners.
when he spoke, the quiet was so loud
that once in a while someone would
feel the need to cough or clear their throat
just to hear it broken, even for just a moment.
he was really only good on the fly,
off the cuff with no script.
he was a marvelous improviser
and that's just what he did when he'd
pull one of his charms on someone.
he knew how to quickly read a man
and get the essence of him locked down.
from there it was simply a matter
of accessing his vast memory files
to pull a tactic most likely to be effective.
he was really best one-on-one,
not that many people that see him
speak that way these days.
with an hour one-to-one in a small room
he could get you to set your family aside,
turn all your thinking upside down and take a bullet for him.

all she wants is a cinnamon pretzel
from the corner vendor
so I dig into my pocket
and fork over the cash,
my seven year old niece
gets her snack and we cruise
down the long aisle of booths
at the San Diego County Fair.
we have to avoid ghost themed rides
because she's recently developed
a phobia of all supernatural ideas.
so we pass on "Ghost Spin"
and "Night of the Living Dead" rides
but she falls absolutely in love
with a brutally jerking roller coaster.
shit! just my luck.
she couldn't like the big modern
safe one that they've recently built
according to the new safety standards.
no, she likes the 20-year-old,
rickety, wooden piece of shit
that even the fair organizers
are trying to figure out how to replace.
she can't get enough of the ride
so we go on it at least six times.
I say at least because I lost count
somewhere after the third or fourth trip.
later as we head over to a photo booth
we notice a small stage
and a group of cheerleaders/dancers
doing a choreographed routine.
my little niece squeals in delight
and starts to dance in time
to the show she's just soaking up.

She opened up the plastic "time capsule"
at the large family party
and pulled out eight or nine pieces of paper.
Each one had hand written notes on it
and was a representation of one family member.
Five years earlier, everyone had been asked,
to write down several predictions, of
where their lives would be in five years.
Some people had written job-related notes
and still others had written hopes or fears.
She popped the cap over cake and ice cream
and pulled out the first entry to the capsule.
It was children's handwriting and cutely,
it spoke of extra toys and time at baseball practice.
The next one was a cousin's and it started
out stating that he'd have $200,000 in the bank.
He smiled at hearing his previous thinking.
It was funny because he has more
than that sum in his account.
He reached over and patted the head of his son.
Another was read and another
and they received cheers and laughter.
Then she pulled out two at once.
She opened one, glanced at it,
folded it and slipped it to me quietly.
Then she smiled at reading the next one
and continued with the process.
I smiled, confused, and opened my entry.
It had two hopes / predictions written on it.
First and foremost, it said that I'd be published
and working in writing with success.
Second, it said my finances would be
under control and that I'd use that money well.
Suddenly, I understood why she'd handed me
the piece of paper with such mystery.

She was saving me a world of embarrassment
having to read such bullshit aloud.

They aren't running because they're happy;
it's a fear that has them so "healthy."
They all fear the same evil man
and no one likes to think about him.
He's always in town, hanging around
looking in on all of his stupid charges.
He can see the fear on their faces
and it makes him snicker to think
of them losing sleep and going grey over him.
He knows he has us all under his thumb
so it's easy for him to smile
when he's looking into someone's eyes.
He's seen all the offers, bribes and begging
for twenty lifetimes so it's a certainty
that it's really not possible to impress him.
He's not a friendly type, a loner really.
I'm not sure people want to be his pal.
It's not like you get anything back
from the shadowy bastard.
It's not like he's clear with you.
He gives hints of his interest and the rest
is in your court so better wake up.
Or you might go to sleep and run into him.
And no one likes to run into him.
Not by day or by night and it's never easy
to experience all he's got alone.
But sometimes it's even harder
to face him with someone you love.
So it's a no-win situation.
Best to just relax, let go and let him
do his damned job.

every color of pill is available
so that now people truly experience
a rainbow of pharmacopeia.
it's just a mood-elevating culture.
or maybe it's a mood-suppressing culture
and everybody is really just
a big energy sack, holding it all in.
it's about lips floating around your mind
and it's about drive-through lovemaking.
give me two hip shakes and a mighty burger
and please don't forget my curly fries.
they'll make it your way but serve it theirs.
I haven't seen the justice everyone's talking about
and I haven't seen the promise everyone's bitching about.
all I've seen is the same old same old
rolling over itself like miserable mulch.
it looks like utter hellish shit
but it'll take and grow and give life.
so people drive by trying to take your door off
and the cops are looking closely for driving errors
and most people have forgotten their children.
they think that money is a connection
to their offspring but they couldn't be more wrong.
we live in the world of the brain menu.
it opens up and has lots of neat colors and in each
square is a list of different options available.
put me here with a little cha-cha
and make it spicy but not fire-breathing evil.
okay?
can't handle that?
well tough.
so snap to.

look deep into my eyes
they're the last you're going to see ever again.
look hard and see that you are done
you are what I call meat;
I've been waiting for this day
for so long that you can
enjoy my smile
it's the last one you're going to see.
ever.
this is the end.
for you.
my end is soon, but not tonight.
this special evening's bloodbath
will be all yours
you could say, you're the guest of honor
you worthless piece of shit.
my wounds are un-healing
and my arms have only one purpose left;
blowing your brains and skull against that there wall.
so even though you can only see hatred
in my eyes and on my face
I suggest you take some pleasure from this face
because in just a few seconds
there will be nothing left of you.
you will be gone.
dead isn't exactly enough to describe
what you're going to be.
I'll incinerate you, your house,
your family, friends and colleagues.
so this terrible smile you're looking at
is a final cigarette for a man
tied to a post before a firing squad if you will.
it's nothing but a new beginning
for you because you know
exactly why I'm here.

you have to have been waiting for this day
for so long now
that there's no way this is a surprise.
no chance.
you have to be slightly relieved
I must think
to finally have this done with.
it brings me no joy, no happiness.
this moment is merely a fact of life,
like the wind and the rain.
what you did to my friend's little girl,
had to be you signing up for this!
that much I do believe.
so let me be the first to tell you
your days of constant worry,
looking over your shoulder,
wondering when it would be coming for you, are over.
so, if it's alright with you,
let's just get down to business,
okay?
okay.

Hollywood couldn't have scripted it,
not the way it all went down.
It's still got most of us stunned.
I'm not sure I'll ever get over it
and if you're ready, sit down.
No really. Sit down and I'll tell you…
She shot her son in the face
when he came home with the
very first "B" grade in his academic career.
He was twelve, in 7th grade
and incredibly bright - all "A's"
since kindergarten. All "A's". Literally.
Until he had to complete auto shop.
He tried his hardest to participate
in the middle school's 7th period
"career prep" course - a new state initiative.
They had him under the hood of
a Ford Mustang and all he had to do
was memorize what everything
was named inside of there.
He just couldn't seem to get his interest
levels high enough to deeply commit
those memorization attempts in his mind.
So, he got a "C" on that test
and was still in range to get an "A" in the class
if he could ace everything else-
but a missing homework assignment
from his folder led to an embarrassing
moment with the shop teacher
who didn't believe the idea
that the homework had simply disappeared
as the boy frantically insisted.
Between the bungled Ford engine test
and the "lying" about the homework,
the shop teacher decided then and there

on a "B" grade for him.
After Mom blew him all over the wall
she shuddered for a moment
and pulled out of her apron pocket,
the missing homework assignment.

he walks out his front door
goes to his beat up car,
trick-starts it with a huff and puff
and drives himself to his morning job.
from six to noon he works bagels,
baking them, storing them,
selling them, throwing them away.
then he goes to the city college,
gets into "school" clothes and does two hours
of his computer engineering 101.
he's just getting started on that.
and math is not one of his strong points.
by three pm he's out of class
and whips over to the factory
where he's a janitor, mopping all night.
at one am he heads towards his house,
eyes blood red and lips cracked dry.
he's so exhausted he's falling asleep
at the wheel and has to run
the air conditioning to stay awake.
he pulls into his neighborhood
fights for a parking spot three blocks away
and marches home with
grocery bags in his tired hands.
he walks through his front door,
sits on his couch alone.
and has one beer, a handful of peanuts
and two pieces of cheddar cheese.
this is his nightly ritual.
he watches the late night talk shows,
goes into his son's room, kisses the boy.
he goes into his daughter's room,
kisses her while she sleeps.
goes into his bedroom, kisses his sleepy wife
and sets his alarm to go off in three hours.

they held Mark's head under the shower
and ran cold water all over him.
they all got wet trying frantically
to revive the young man.
Tony turned to Sara and said
"slap him…the son of a bitch…"
she was more scared than she'd ever
been in her entire life but she did it.
she slapped Mark's face - nothing.
no response at all as water sprayed
down over all their actions.
their clothes were soaking through.
"he's o-d-ing, man," Sara cried out.
"yeah. yeah. you're right."
"we gotta get him an ambulance."
"but they'll find all the drugs, the pipes,
the guns… that other shit, too," Tony whined.
"look at him."
Mark's head flopped around like a ragdoll's.
Sara peeled one of his eyelids back
and saw his eyeball twitching rapidly.
"fuck me!!" exclaimed Tony in horror.
"shit…he's going, man. this ain't cool."
"you call the ambulance."
"how?"
"911, dipshit! quick!!"
Sara ran out of the shower to the phone.
she started dialing it in.
"you are going to be okay, pal," Tony
whispered like a father into Mark's ear.
"you are a good guy and it's not your time,
so hang in there pal. okay pal? please.
look…I need you to listen to me…
you gotta come back…please, pal…hang on…"

they climbed into his car
and drove down the coast
he kept a hand on her thigh
for the entire ride
and she loved that
they fucked all night
and kissed all morning
they'd found one another
at a strange little bookstore
and had been inseparable since
they barely knew each other
but already they had trips
to foreign lands planned
they didn't want to
go back to Los Angeles
they were happier in San Diego
and in Mexico with no schedules
and no idiots from their pasts
stamping and stumbling about
they were looking merely
for a ripe piece of sun
to lay their hope down on
they were floating in
a dream and neither wanted
it to stop or change at all
their time together
was like a favorite song
you want to play it
over and over and over
and nothing can satisfy
but that song
at full volume

he grows out of their bodies
because he feeds on their insides.
he enters them at touch
and becomes them or seems to.
then slowly he devours all
the blood, the veins, the bones,
the meat and with a supernatural
energy keeps their skin filled out.
but when he's eaten all there is
he leaves; he moves to
the next body and the one he's leaving
just crumples to the floor
like a sack just emptied.
he delights in watching this happen
from the eyes of his new host body.
often times he even plays
with the shed skin
like a child playing with a snake skin…
then he's back to his m.o.
keep things quiet; keep them cool.
he wants no attention at all.
he'll call in sick,
stay away from others
while he can consume the new
body's resources in peace.
if he can do it all inside
their home he'll do it that way.
he only ventures out into the world
when his food supply is running
low and he's in need of fresh human.
the first steps out of the front door
when he has to go on a new hunt
are always rather tentative.

he took his sandals off,
tossed them by the rear door
and then took her hand
and they headed down to the beach.
they were quiet, at peace
as they walked out
across the sandy dunes.
a gorgeous day greeted them
and they made their way
down to the shore's edge.
they wet their feet
and continued their walk
in near total silence.
when they did stop moving
he ran a hand over her face
and she laughed at him.
what was he doing?
he ran a hand through her hair
and really kissed her forehead
with a deep love pouring
out of his every fiber.
then she understood.
it hit her like a ton of bricks
and she immediately,
without a single sound
began to cry, tears streaming
down her face uncontrollably.
she looked at him,
trying to be as brave as he
but she found it hard.
how could she have forgotten?
today was his visit
to the doctor
for the test results.

she was everything he'd ever need:
all legs and tits and an ass from heaven.
she was well-groomed and fashionable.
she never let anyone see her frown.
it was as if that was forbidden.
she was determined to appear
as all upside and little downside.
conversationally, she was a wizard.
an actual studied scholar
who could turn words on a dime
and spin them into other uses.
she couldn't be caught off guard
and when she was,
she covered it so well with cleverness
that no one ever noticed
but him.
he saw her downside,
as small as it was
and fell deeply, passionately in love
with her as he realized
that he did have a special connection
with her that she was unaware of.
he too could hide expertly
behind varied words
spewed at varied tempos.
he too was not often caught
seeming off guard or taken aback.
nothing could shock him.
he had a leader's face
and she a queen's.
so he relaxed when she left the room
heading for a vacation with another man.
he knew, with no sense of false hope,
that she would indeed be back.

The middle-aged woman came running out
screaming and freaking out.
The American soldiers aimed
their machine guns at the burqa-wearing lady
who kept pointing toward her house.
Two large homes exploded
into millions of small shards
only some two blocks away.
"What do you think, man?"
asked Danny, a 19-year-old kid
from New Jersey.
"She's got one hand hidden,
her left hand is in her fucking skirts,"
replied a frantic Federico,
a Cuban lad from Hollywood, Florida.
"She's trying to fuck with us."
"I can't tell," said Fed.
"Stay back ma'am!" cried Danny.
"She won't stop coming," said Fed.
"Get your hands out, bitch!"
"Get your hands out!!"
They shot her to pieces
and each one would later
say it felt like shooting their own mothers.
The Arab woman slumped
to the dirt with twenty
steaming bullet holes in her.
The children came running
from her house, crying and yelling
with genuine pain.
Danny used the barrel of his gun
to flip the lady's robes open
as her children surrounded her dead body.
They could see the woman's hand trying
to reach the pin of
a Russian-made, heavy shrapnel, hand grenade.

it's probably her tan stomach
that first pops into my head
when I wake up
and I head out my front door
into the long, hotel hallway,
walk over to her door
and knock with strong punctuations.
she comes to the door,
still groggy since the sun
isn't even up yet
and looks at me confused
but with the most lovely smile.
a smile only her lips
could form - so utterly full
and inviting while being so natural.
she gives me a quizzical look
accentuated by an arched eyebrow
and I answer the only way I can think of.
I leap in and kiss her.
then I pull back to read her reactions…
surprise. confusion. shock!
oh no…maybe this is wrong. too much, too fast.
then she breaks out laughing
and grabs me with all her might.
she squeezes me with the most
loving hug I've ever gotten.
we sit in that tacky, dimly-lit hall
kissing in the most innocent way
for over an hour and a half.
two bellboys walk by,
looking on and ogling
but we don't notice.
it's only later that my
peripheral vision memory lets me know
that they were even there.

The overjoyed look on her face
as she keeps her eyes on mine
lets me know that she's
in a mood to get crazy tonight.
She's prancing around the dance floor,
flirting with two suave black men
while keeping her gaze locked with mine,
as I stand just outside and above
the throng of sweaty flesh.
She bounces her ample ass
from side to side, running her hands
along the sides of her body.
She sways and shakes
and lets her short bob cut
flop to and fro with the rhythm.
Her face gives hints of
what we will again do tonight.
I can see the groans and grunts,
the ooohs, the oh nos and the
Oh My Fucking Gods.
They are all there on her
gorgeous face, beginning to bead
with sweat from all her wiggling.
She's completely electric
and pulsing and throbbing in every way.
She's far more than just sexual
and sexy and model-good-looking.
She's intriguing and unknown
in the right ways and her eyes
turn me on quicker than her
agile, curved hips.
So when she disappoints her dancer/suitors
on the floor to cut out and head over to me
I'm not the least bit surprised
but I'm still sufficiently thrilled.

she accompanied her girlfriend
the first time and watched mostly;
how she hooked a john,
got him to come up to the motel
and got him to drop every penny
in his wallet and ATM.
Tina, the blonde goddess had
been making money for three years
and was really trying to make
a significant difference in Diana's life.
the first guy Diana watched
was Tony Jones…a Texan
stuck in New York who loved fat steaks
and women with curves.
Tina got him up to her usual room
but when he came in
and saw Diana, dressed demurely,
sitting in a corner watching TV
he was a little taken aback.
Tina explained that this was her friend
who was learning the biz
and just wanted to watch them.
Tony calmed down enough to
get naked and get on the bed
but he couldn't stop looking over
at the cute, curious girl in the corner.
that was how she knew
she would be good at being a pro.
she felt it right then.
the way Tony looked at her
with utter lust in his bloodshot eyes.
she got up, got undressed
and hopped into the action
without a single word.

She exploded into flames spontaneously
and ran out of her bedroom screaming
as she burned alive.
She ran into the living room
and looked at her miserable parents.
"You pieces of shit are coming with me,"
she cried out as her face blistered
from the flames consuming her body.
She ran over to her horrified parents
and hopped on them, spreading the flames
until they too were lit up and screaming.
She looked to the ceiling, to the sky
that must have been just beyond it.
"Why God…why me?" she asked weakly.
Just then the front door opened
and her ex-boyfriend walked in
with his new piece of ass.
They got the flame treatment
and went down in terror-filled fashion.
"I'm almost dead," she said as she stood
looking at the bodies of the two dead couples.
She looked over at the television
and a lousy, predictable cop show came on.
"I hate that show!!"
She jumped on the television and killed it too.
So as she came to the end, she stumbled
into the bathroom to try to hop in the shower
to extinguish the fire that was raging
from her feet to the ceiling as she kept burning
and burning and so on.
Just before she could turn the faucet knob,
she noticed her box of wing-tipped tampons.
"I hate those fucking tampons," she said,
and burned them up too and it was one moment
longer than she could handle.

So that was how they found her:
burnt to a crisp and scowling at her tampons.

They want to know when he met her
and how their little affair began.
He started slowly at first,
explaining in that interrogation room
everything he could remember about her.
He'd been teaching at a small state college
and she was one of his brightest
English students, actually going
out of her way to learn more than assigned.
She had stayed one day
after all the other students had left
and decided to push things forward.
She was not very coy how she
shut the door with a bang
and then dropped her books to the floor,
and then started to come over to him.
She licked her ruby lips and even
loosened her shirt's top button
in a very forward signal to him.
He had kissed her there
with all of the passion he'd bottled up,
thinking he'd never get to act on any of it.
While he simply had wanted to kiss
she had wanted even more.
She had taken off all of her clothes,
lay on top of his wooden desk
and begun to masturbate her pussy.
He had started to stroke his cock
and then he went down on her.
He had eaten her for an hour
before he even looked up
long enough to notice his wife
standing near the classroom door,
.45 in hand, aimed at the girl.

She's got the tents and a truck
so she's got me heading up
to some pretty mountains for camping.
We get to the campgrounds,
pay a small fee and go to our spot.
Then we spend the next hour
getting up our tent and a fire
and a few Coleman cooking wonders.
As sun sets, I've got a soup on
and she's made eggplant sandwiches.
These sandwiches are so good
they actually make me smile.
After a nice meal, a smoke and coffee
we go into our tent
and she undresses slowly, seductively.
Then she's on her knees
sucking my cock with a fury.
She's on fire and I love it.
I'm pulling on her hair,
sticking fingers inside of her
and she's getting me incredibly hard.
She's got tiny tits and a great ass
and before long she's riding me.
We're making all kinds of noise
when I hear a voice at the zipped-up
tent door, "Hello…hello in there?" a woman asks.
"Uh…yes?" I ask, slowing the sex down.
"We're in the space next to yours
and we were wondering if
the two of you were here for
the swingers camping trip
or were you just normal folks
who didn't know we were having
a getaway weekend up here?" she asked.
We unzipped and let her in,

let her join us for the night
and talked to her in the morning.

She put on her black slip
and came out of the bathroom
with each hand on a hip.
She gave a hip tilt,
shook her long, dark brown hair
and gave me these eyes
that burned into me deeply.
I couldn't look away.
Slowly she came over to me
laying quietly on the bed
and she licked her lips purposefully.
Before she came to the edge
of the bed she paused,
turned around and began to dance
to the Latin jazz on the stereo.
She put her hips to all their use.
The slip's lacy frill barely
covered the full roundness of her ass.
She knew exactly what she
was doing to me and she delighted
in doing it which only
turned me on that much more.
I was twisting around in my skin
just trying to be cool.
I wanted to keep a cool.
She'd enjoy it more that way.
So, with a slowness feigning disinterest
I stood up and headed towards the bathroom.
When she saw me pass her
she gasped aloud, confused.
Without a moment's hesitation,
I scooped her up into my arms,
leaped onto the bed with her
bouncing all around
and then I kissed her like I meant it.

he was busted by the cops
the first time for being involved
in a weight loss powder pyramid scheme,
he was the vice-president
of the totally phony company
that signed up plenty of sales affiliates
at around $500 a pop
even though they had no actual product.
the second time he was running
a computer scam where he
contacted people at random via e-mail/spam
and lied saying he was a lawyer
who had recently been appointed
to distribute the gains of a will
of a distant relative who had
supposedly just died in a foreign hospital.
mostly people deleted his crap e-mails
but once in a while, a desperate person
would call up and pay his $800 "legal fee"
in order to receive their promised check
for well over $10,000.
needless to say those checks never arrived.
the "office address" he gave people was
ultimately nothing but a bus depot.
but one of his victims actually
took it upon himself to bust the slime ball.
the victim hired a private detective,
drove across two states, staked out
three residences for two weeks
and finally was able to call law enforcement in.
as he passed the victim, in handcuffs,
the con man exclaimed, "Jesus, you took it so personal.
why'd you have to take it so fucking personal?"

I stood up and bullets flew
exploding everything around me.
"Come and get me," I taunted
and then dropped back down
taking cover from the three killers.
The leader was an excellent shot
and his cronies' main asset
was their sheer stupidity and brazenness.
These two would charge into anything.
That's why I was having to act
so ultra-macho and challenging.
Normally in a gun fight I don't talk.
I just aim and shoot and duck.
But these monkeys had me cornered
in the back of a West L.A. gymnasium.
Members who were working out
all fled after the first shot was fired.
Luckily the idiots bit
and got hot under the collar
at my cavalier attitude
and they charged creeping low
but they charged down the two aisles.
I stayed on the ground, took my aim
through the most insane jungle
of metallic parts of workout equipment.
They came ever closer and I smiled.
Both men's ankles came into view.
I shot the hell out of both of them.
They went down screaming, freaking.
The leader hesitated. He didn't do anything.
"What's the matter, shithead? You ain't shit
without your muscle? Come and get me," I said.
The moron actually thought the emotion I displayed
was real, he bit, he misplayed and died too.

she gets in the Mercedes
and gives him a blowjob,
then she gets her $100
and heads back out onto the street.
after getting $400
she quits for the night,
gets a little motel room
and goes over to the diner;
she gets steak and eggs
and has three beers,
she belches loudly at
a church-going family
passing through the aisle
trying to get to the register.
suddenly a hand slaps her.
it's one of her johns,
who's in the diner
and saw her harass the family.
"you little bitch," he growls.
"fuck you, you limp dick," she fires back.
this really pisses him off;
he chases her all around
the diner until security comes
and grabs her and holds her.
the john beats her again
and then leaves at the request
of a fairly reasonable security guard.
"you're much too much
of a real woman to treat
yourself with this kind of
disrespect and mindlessness.
this ain't for you."
it's the first person
who's ever said anything like that
to her with genuineness in his eyes

and right then, right there,
she promptly quits pro-ing
and never goes back
always reassured in her decision
by playing his words
in her head
over and over again

I didn't want to think about you ever again
so I locked you away in a small box and stuffed it
into the furthest recess in my mind that I could find.
I had become sick thinking excessively of you;
all I could see in my head at night was you;
images of you – blinking in my brain at night.
it was absolutely unending how I could go over it;
the way we ended.
I was really smoking more than I ever have
and we know that's really saying something.
I wasn't in the sturdiest frame of mind;
the slightest things could set me off on a tear –
some things would just make me instantly depressed;
like seeing the old bar we'd drink at
or the restaurant where we first kissed.
some things would make me instantly pissed off;
like thinking about how you played me
or thinking about how I gave you my all.
you got elements of me I haven't ever given anyone;
you had me thinking we could make it all the way,
finish the long race together.
but I'm also prone to utter fantasy.

it's never too late
for you to find your way home
and to be a REAL creature under
skies built on what we are beneath
the skinny skins we wear
like ill-conceived fashions
fashioned on the one and only enemy
with devious designs meant to test us –
the only beast that can hold us
in our self-made prisons –
that awful but weak monster:
FEAR.
you are so much more than that,
you are so much beyond your own
ability to perceive;
you are the saving,
you are the light in darkest tunnels unreal,
it is you who is meant for the big turn.
and it has always been there,
that brilliant illumination
that only you can take shine away from.
it is you
and has always been you
with the infinite bursting
from your own fingertips.
it's never too late to be
the very thing you have lied
to yourself that you didn't deserve to be;
to be the whole and the entire of
what you have made yourself believe
was nothing more than a dream;
it is you that you have been waiting for;
it is you who isn't the mistake
but who has been mistaken in the mirror,
taking yourself down

again and again with a grotesque agenda
invented in a place that doesn't exist –
if you could be honest with yourself.
you are what can remain if
you had the courage today
to stand up to yourself –
your false self;
the self you work so hard to keep up.
doesn't it seem absurd how much
effort it takes to hold that face up?
to keep blowing up the same awful
balloon (escaped zoo) animal?
to keep lying when your mouth
doesn't want to even help you anymore?
it hasn't passed by…
not yet, not yet it hasn't.
why can they still suspect you,
your inner demons
if you haven't already betrayed them
by being real?
don't be afraid
like you've been so many times
like you've been when you couldn't control it
or let yourself believe you couldn't.
don't give in to it
that stupid, small, incorrect fear.
don't let it win again.
don't be what you know
is not you.
don't do it.
don't.
be the one you actually are.
this time, don't let the unchangeable past
let you make another wrong move –
not when you have finally figured out
what you are supposed to do.
not now.
not now, goddamn it!
not now.
enough.

that way is over.
that way of being.
that way of letting yourself believe
that this world is nothing
and that your actions don't matter.
that is over now.
ask, ask!!
do you believe at all in that
untrue excuse that the world
is simply death and betrayal?
you know that you don't.
you know how fortunate you are.
you know it deep in there
deep where there are no barriers
deep inside where you protect
the child that everyone of us still is
underneath all the trappings.
look there and don't take your eyes away.
look
look
look at you.
don't call the 'day' 'night'
when it is clearly day.
enough. enough.
time to be happy.
time to be poor, hardworking, stressed and overwhelmed
by this gift/job/miracle/reward/essence -
time…to…be…happy…
the real happy.
the deep happy.
the true happy.
it isn't too late and you know it
that's what keeps you up nights
and keeps you down days
makes you a colander of spaghetti
on two feet.
and if you'd just believe
like you used to believe
it wouldn't be this hard –
as hard as you make it on yourself.

you've been in a cave
and you haven't let yourself out
long enough to let your eyes adjust;
it's not too late –
!!???**!!!+=-$$???!!...?!!!!!!!
it's not too late...I keep
reminding...myself:
it's not too late...
to be the father he deserves.

you lift me up
and make me something new
something I never saw in myself,
you take me up
to a place in the clouds
that men only dream of;
you are the only one
who has gotten me into this state
this way
this self
and I just can't believe
that you don't want to talk to me,
that you don't wonder
how it is that we are not together.
don't you want to talk to me?
be in my arms
and be held like you know
I have wanted to hold you since
the very first time I saw you?
we had such a life-changing time –
it couldn't have just been me.
you started a fire
but you are afraid of the heat.
and I know that I don't deserve
to have your light shine on me
but I can't accept this
not inside – where I really am.
it was a special thing.
I think it is a special thing
that I cannot let go of.
I am not sure of much
but this I am.
no one can replace you
no one can give me
any of the delights you

brought to my very soul.
when you are around, I am changed
lifted
up
and taken to the giddy place of hypnotic
calm that only your face can take me.

the first time I choked her
I was so afraid I'd hurt her
that I didn't really do it right.
she liked being touched, kissed, licked
then fucked and finally slam-fucked and choked out
until she'd smile as she came.
we were unable to keep our hands off one another
anytime we were in the same room.
this made things difficult for us both
as we were not exactly show-off, PDA-types.
we were simply drawn together like metal
to magnet instantly and forcefully.
I always had a thing for her
that was emotional and physical all at once,
and nothing I could do could get
her out of my mind.
we started out fucking in my car
in the parking lot of the bank
next to my favorite bar, The Bulldog, in Monterey,
and it just heated up from there.
her cheeks would get so red when I'd touch
her arm that it was as if a Tesla coil
had been turned on at full power –
the electricity was actually alive in the air
all around us.
we'd do our best to act like anything else mattered
but it was all a game, us pretending
that we were doing anything other than
simply waiting until we could be alone.
a day was empty when she was away
and a night was a nightmare when we
couldn't sleep in the same bed.
it was hyper-sexual but it was so much more
than just that.
we were two halves of one whole

and it is fair to say I lived
for the moment we were finally alone.
being with her never got old or tired
or routine or simple.
there was a laugh-filled playfulness
balanced by an intense submission-based sex
that made her nearly crush me
every time we'd sit down on the couch
because she'd nearly sit on me
even as we were just watching TV.
in bed, it was that super-love
that is supposed to be just in songs,
unreal and fantastical.
she needed to be tied up and blindfolded
and I needed to shove her face into the pillow
and spank her as she would grind her hips
and play with herself,
inviting me to take over that duty.
the smile on her face as the blindfold
would go on, I cannot get out of my face even now.
she was the one who led me into the S&M.
I was never really a bondage guy.
really.
but she loved it and the more she loved it,
the more I came to love it.
all she had to do was cross her wrists
out in public
and I got the bondage reference and couldn't
stop staring at her.
it was awful. it was beautiful.
it was everything.
it still is.
we finally got to the point that she asked me
to put my hand around her neck
and lightly feign choking her
right when she was about to come.
it would push her over the edge.
and that smile;
the smile she'd almost laugh out
when she was coming with

my hand around her throat,
still owns me.
owns me.
I am not my own man.
it is a simple fact of life.
I still belong to her.
I still belong to that frightening,
all-consuming fire of a love
that nearly burned us both up.
I pray and wish and scream her name
and then wake up and understand
that we are not together now.
I am owned by someone who won't
speak to me, see me, or take my calls.
I am owned.
once before, we broke up
and we didn't talk to one another
for about a year,
and when we finally spoke and met eyes
after all that time
I knew I had to tell her how miserable
it had been when we were apart.
I had to just say it outright
unafraid, hopeful that it would reach
across the divide of all that time away
from each other.
I had to tell her that when we had
been done, were finished,
my life had come to mean
absolutely nothing at all.
so I stood before her that time
and I started, "when we ended—"
she cut me off.
"we never ended," she said.
and her words echo in my head
every day now.
every night
and even when I am asleep.
"we never ended."

It's all a big lie
that I'm doing okay
I tell myself when the long, long night
keeps stretching on out.
I cannot find my way
to my bed because it just
looks so damned empty I want to die.
I'm alone in a crowd of my friends
wondering if anything will
make me forget your smell –
that sweet, sweet scent around your neck.
I can't find any form of relief
and nothing looks promising anymore;
I think maybe I'm shrinking
falling down to a lower place,
a little kid's seat in the corner;
a self-imposed dunce cap my newest fashion statement.
I can't hold back much longer now,
I just know I'm breaking down –
I mean, I'm going to find you,
and try to get through to you;
try to find anything to make you
look at me like you used to.
I'm simply nothing now – not a speck –
I'm just a big lump of meat
taking up far too much space,
I can't breathe sometimes –
in fact, I can't breathe at all, ever.
People are talking to me
and I think they think I'm rude
because I can't hear anything anymore.
I love movies – they're my favorite thing
but now I just stare through the screen
and the popcorn that I have dreamed of
every time I head to a movie theater

is tasteless and a waste and just nothing.
Like everything is nothing now.
I'm confused about everything;
and I'm nothing if not decisive –
or, I was – I used to be.
Now my shit's just all falling apart,
every part is crumbling;
not just the important ones
but all of them – even the small ones.
I won't be able to keep this distance
too much longer.
I'm worried I'll seem like a stalker
but I think I really am going to
break down and start twitching like
an epileptic man seizing if I don't see you –
and I do mean, just "see" you.
It goes without saying that I want so much more
than to simply lay eyes upon you,
but I am not sure I'm going to resist
these waves of energy that make me do
some of the oddest things I've ever
found myself doing.
And I really am finding myself doing them;
As if I'm waking up from a dream
but I'm behind the wheel
driving towards your house
up on that mountain where your
whole family hates me and would
probably shoot me on sight.
Or I wake up and I'm at the music store
where you used to love to go buy sheet music;
Or I wake up and I'm driving in circles
around a park we'd sit in, kissing.
I want to know what it is I'm
supposed to do now.
No one can tell me, help me –
I've never felt like this before,
so certain of my loss.
I've had a couple real relationships
and lost them but in one case,

I wanted it to end and was happier;
and in the other, I didn't want the end
and I was angry – but I was so angry,
it was a clear tip-off that that girl
was not the one meant for me.
But this, now, here, where I find myself –
is somewhere without any precedent for me
to refer back to as a guidepost.
God, I'm a mess – and I think I hide it well
from my parents, my friends, my co-workers.
It actually kind of makes me sick
that the world just keeps on turning
and you're not here.
I really feel like it should stop spinning;
or do something different – to reflect this horror.
But no one is moving around me at a pace
any different than they did before,
it's as if I am dead inside but still walking;
that's it.
I'm dead inside now.
I feel ready for the mortician to make me up
and prepare my pine box.
I want to crawl inside it and shut the lid
and close my eyes for a long time.
Because maybe I could turn this all
into just some bad dream.
That's it!
That's the answer.
It has to be. This just can't be the real truth.
I'm just dreaming that last groggy part
of a crazy, fear-inspired misrepresentation
of the real, waking world.
Right! I should have known…a fear dream.
That's all. Has to be…
Here I go…
I'm going to find everything all right again…
Here I go…
I just know you'll be there when I open my eyes…
Here I go…
I'm going to wake up any minute now…

ABOUT THE AUTHOR

Carlos de los Rios is one of the leading writers of the contemporary underground California literary scene. He has written several books of prose and poetry that have landed him a reputation as a cutting edge storyteller. His weekly online satire goldenpunch.com (which has been called a "literary Doonesbury" by critics) has frequently put his work at the center of the American political conversation. He has also written acclaimed feature films for Academy Award-winners and nominees Lauren Bacall, Elliott Gould and Harvey Fierstein, among others. He resides in California.

Made in the USA
Las Vegas, NV
20 July 2021

26741932R00105